Praise for Preteen Zone

"Life comes hard and fast at today's preteens. To help guide them through the chaos, Preteen Zone tells the story of four diverse preteens and the real-world challenges they face—like struggles at home, struggles at school, and struggles to believe in a God they can't see. True-to-life examples and thoughtful questions encourage readers to turn to God for the answers they need. And the unique storytelling approach is sure to keep them turning the pages!"

Tama Fortner
ECPA award-winning and bestselling author
of more than sixty titles

"In Preteen Zone, Mary-Lynn Chambers offers a scriptural guide to preteens as they navigate one of childhood's most formative and challenging stages. With a perfect balance of scripture and relevant preteen experiences, this devotional equips preteens with a God-centered approach to youthful Christian living. This is a must-read every preteen!"

Rockwell Dundas
Vice President, Philanthropy, World Vision Canada

"Preteen Zone is a wonderful resource to encourage kids in their journey with God. Weaving together the stories of four friends and their everyday lives, Mary-Lynn Chambers draws young readers in with relatable characters and believable circumstances. The accompanying questions are valuable for both personal reflection and group discussions."

Diana Lawrence
Designer of kids books, B&H Publishing Group

"In this extraordinary preteen devotional, Dr. Chambers leads the reader on a God-centered, Scripture-based, and prayer-focused journey that shows how God fits within the challenging, inquisitive, and adventurous Preteen Zone of life. It is an honor to offer my hearty endorsement of such a practical and timely work for today's young people."

Dr. Scott Adams
Pastor and Youth Ministry Professor at Regent University

Mary-Lynn Chambers

DEVOTIONS
FOR
PRETEENS AGES
EIGHT TO TWELVE

AMBASSADOR INTERNATIONAL
GREENVILLE, SOUTH CAROLINA & BELFAST, NORTHERN IRELAND

www.ambassador-international.com

Preteen Zone
DEVOTIONS FOR PRETEENS AGES EIGHT TO TWELVE

©2025 by Mary-Lynn Chambers
All rights reserved

Hardcover ISBN: 978-1-64960-886-4
Paperback ISBN: 978-1-64960-631-0
eISBN: 978-1-64960-680-8

No part of this publication may be reproduced, distributed, or transmitted in any form or by any means, including photocopying, recording, or other electronic or mechanical methods, without the prior written permission of the publisher, except in the case of brief quotations embodied in critical reviews and certain other noncommercial uses permitted by copyright law. For permission requests, contact the publisher using the information below.

Cover design by Karen Slayne
Interior typesetting by Karen Slayne
Edited by Sydney Witbeck
Illustrations by Mario de Belda Cid

Scripture marked NIV taken from Holy Bible, New International Version®, NIV® Copyright ©1973, 1978, 1984, 2011 by Biblica, Inc.® Used by permission. All rights reserved worldwide.

Scripture marked NLT taken from Holy Bible, New Living Translation, copyright © 1996, 2004, 2015 by Tyndale House Foundation. Used by permission of Tyndale House Publishers, Inc., Carol Stream, Illinois 60188. All rights reserved.

AMBASSADOR INTERNATIONAL
Emerald House
411 University Ridge, Suite B14
Greenville, SC 29601
United States
www.ambassador-international.com

AMBASSADOR BOOKS
The Mount
2 Woodstock Link
Belfast, BT6 8DD
Northern Ireland, United Kingdom
www.ambassadormedia.co.uk

The colophon is a trademark of Ambassador, a Christian publishing company.

To my amazing grandchildren

Marlowe, Fletcher, Myles

Teller and Kohen

Never stop discovering more
about our great God!

Love, Bibi

TABLE OF CONTENTS

Day 1   My God is Able 15

Day 2   My God is Abounding in Love 17

Day 3   My God is Abundantly Good 19

Day 4   My God is Accepting 21

Day 5   My God is Active 23

Day 6   My God is Alive 25

Day 7   My God is Almighty 27

Day 8   My God is Approachable 29

Day 9   My God is My Atonement 31

Day 10 My God is Attentive 35

Day 11 My God is Avenging 37

Day 12	My God is Awesome	39
Day 13	My God is Beautiful	41
Day 14	My God is Blameless	43
Day 15	My God is a Blessing	45
Day 16	My God is the Bread of Life	47
Day 17	My God is the Breath of Life	49
Day 18	My God is Brilliant	53
Day 19	My God is the Builder	55
Day 20	My God is Calling	59
Day 21	My God is Caring	61
Day 22	My God is Compassionate	63
Day 23	My God is Compelling	67
Day 24	My God is Concerned	71
Day 25	My God is My Conqueror	75
Day 26	My God is Consistent	79
Day 27	My God is Convicting	81

Day 28 My God is the Cornerstone 85

Day 29 My God is My Counselor 89

Day 30 My God is My Creator 91

Day 31 My God is Dazzling 93

Day 32 My God is My Defender 95

Day 33 My God is Delighted 99

Day 34 My God is My Deliverer 101

Day 35 My God is Displeased 103

Day 36 My God is Divine 107

Day 37 My God is Encouraging 109

Day 38 My God is Enthroned 111

Day 39 My God is Equipping 115

Day 40 My God is Eternal 117

Day 41 My God is Everlasting 119

Day 42 My God is Exalted 121

Day 43 My God is Faithful 123

Day 44	My God is My Father	125
Day 45	My God is To Be Feared	127
Day 46	My God is Flawless	129
Day 47	My God is Forgiving	131
Day 48	My God is My Friend	133
Day 49	My God is Giving	135
Day 50	My God is Glorified	137
Day 51	My God is Good	139
Day 52	My God is Gracious	141
Day 53	My God is Great	145
Day 54	My God is My Healer	147
Day 55	My God is My Helper	149
Day 56	My God is Holy	151
Day 57	My God is Immortal	155
Day 58	My God is My Intercessor	157
Day 59	My God is Invisible	159

Day 60	My God is Jealous	161
Day 61	My God is Jesus	165
Day 62	My God is My Judge	169
Day 63	My God is Just	171
Day 64	My God is Kind	173
Day 65	My God is King	175
Day 66	My God is Life-Giving	177
Day 67	My God is Light	181
Day 68	My God Lives	183
Day 69	My God is Lord	185
Day 70	My God is Majestic	187
Day 71	My God is Marvelous	189
Day 72	My God is Merciful	181
Day 73	My God is a Mystery	195
Day 74	My God is Patient	197
Day 75	My God is Peace	199

Day 76	My God is Perfect	201
Day 77	My God is Present	203
Day 78	My God is My Provider	205
Day 79	My God is My Reality	207
Day 80	My God is Reconciling	209
Day 81	My God is My Redeemer	211
Day 82	My God is My Refuge	213
Day 83	My God is My Rest	215
Day 84	My God is Righteous	217
Day 85	My God is My Ruler	219
Day 86	My God is My Savior	221
Day 87	My God is My Shepherd	223
Day 88	My God is My Shield	225
Day 89	My God is Sovereign	227
Day 90	My God is My Strength	229
Day 91	My God is My Teacher	231

Day 92	My God is Trustworthy	233
Day 93	My God is Truth	235
Day 94	My God is Unfailing	237
Day 95	My God is Upright	239
Day 96	My God is Victorious	241
Day 97	My God is Wise	243
Day 98	My God is Wonderful	245
Day 99	My God is Worthy	247
Day 100	My God is Zealous	249
About the Author		251

Day 1
MY GOD IS ABLE

Read: Ephesians 3:20

The knot in Kaylin's stomach tightened as she kicked at a stone lying in her path. It was the first day of school, and she was facing it on her own. Kaylin's straight black hair fell around her face as she shuffled along the sidewalk. With a heavy sigh, she tried talking to God.

"My parents don't care. My friends don't text back. God, when I became a Christian, I thought You would fix everything. So why am I so afraid to go back to school? Why do I feel so alone?"

A honk startled Kaylin out of her slump. She whipped around just as Avery popped her blonde head out of the car window.

"Jump in, Kaylin. We'll take you to school."

"Thanks," Kaylin said as she climbed into the car, "I didn't want to go to school on my own. Did you get my text?"

"Yeah, sorry. We got in late last night. I meant to text you this morning. Sorry, I forgot," Avery explained.

A sigh escaped Kaylin as she flopped against the back seat. "I'm not ready for school to start."

Both Avery and her mom laughed as they spied Glenwood Middle School. Mrs. McPherson, wanting to encourage Kaylin, reminded both girls, "God is able to do great things for you in this school year ... new teachers ... new adventures—"

"Yeah," interrupted Avery, "you've got God, and you've got me. And school is going to be great!"

Kaylin laughed at Avery's silly grin as Mrs. McPherson came to a stop in front of the school. Just then, a basketball bounced off the hood of the car.

"Hey, Aaron," Avery yelled as she climbed out of the car, "I found your basketball!"

Trevor hooked his backpack over one shoulder as he followed Aaron to the McPhersons' car. Aaron grabbed the basketball as the school bell rang.

"Sorry, Mrs. McPherson, I am getting ready for tryouts."

The four friends joined the mass of students entering Glenwood. Kaylin felt much better as she hit Aaron's basketball out of his hand.

"Hopefully your defense gets better now that you're back in school!" Kaylin teased.

> *Now to him who is able to do immeasurably more than all we ask or imagine according to his power that is at work within us.*
>
> *Ephesians 3:20*

What About You?

When has God made a situation better than you thought it would be? Like . . .

- When you visited a new group and found a new friend?

- When you started a chore and found you had fun?

- When something simple became something special?

Take Time to Pray!

Choose a time when God did more than you hoped for. Thank Him for being a God Who is able to do so much more than you thought possible.

Day 2
MY GOD IS ABOUNDING IN LOVE

Read: Psalm 103:8

The screen door slammed behind Trevor, announcing his return from the first day of school.

"I'm back," he called, hoping his mom was home, in a good mood, and ready to hear his announcement.

His mom appeared in the doorway of the kitchen and took a drag on her cigarette; then she slowly blew the smoke off to one side. Folding her arms across her chest, she leaned against the doorframe. Leveling an icy stare at her son, she said, "I see you took as much time to choose your outfit as you did to clean your room this morning."

"Yeah, Mom, good to see you, too." Trevor groaned. "Oh, and by the way, I had a great first day at school."

Trevor's mom moved to the coffee table, where she flicked ashes into a bowl half-filled with old butts. Turning back to Trevor, she retorted, "I've put in long hours at the restaurant so that you can have a roof over your head and food on the table. I've spent all day there cleaning up after slobs, and I don't want to come home and clean up after you, too."

Trevor shot back, "Hey, I should count myself lucky just to have a parent show up at home." He stormed down the hall and slammed his bedroom door behind him. Through the closed door, he could still hear his mom yelling at him.

"It wasn't me who left—it was your dad. I hate the life I have; but I have no choice, and neither do you. So clean up your room!"

Trevor threw himself on his bed. "Home, sweet home—yeah, this is the life. I wonder if anybody loves me."

> *The LORD is compassionate and gracious,*
> *slow to anger, abounding in love.*
> Psalm 103:8

What About You?

At this point in these devotions, Trevor doesn't know God or God's love. Do you know God and His love? God loves you, even when you are not feeling loved by those around you.

Like . . .

- When a friend puts you down, God's Word says you are "wonderfully made" (Psalm 139:14)?

- When someone impatiently yells at you, remember God's "love is patient" (I Cor. 13:4)?

- When you are feeling left out, remember that God wants to be your Friend (John 15:14)?

Take Time to Pray!

Thank God for His abounding love toward you, no matter what your circumstances. Ask God to help you to have the same love for Him and others.

Day 3

MY GOD IS ABUNDANTLY GOOD

Read: Psalm 145:7

"Mr. March!" Coach Ryder's voice boomed above the noise filling the halls of Glenwood Middle School. Aaron whipped around; an eager smile spread across his face. "I've been watching your basketball-playing during gym class. You have what it takes to make the team. Tryouts start next week. Make sure you're there."

Aaron grinned as Coach Ryder strode toward the gym.

"Some guys get all the breaks," Trevor complained as he dropped his backpack at Aaron's feet. Aaron slapped Trevor on his back and turned to open his locker.

"This isn't a lucky break. I'm telling you, man, I prayed about this one," Aaron insisted.

Trevor moved in closer, his face screwed up in disgust. "Don't say that word so loud."

"What word?"

"Prayed," hissed Trevor.

"Hey, God has been good to me in so many ways. I'm not afraid to talk about it," explained Aaron.

Trevor whipped his head from side to side, making sure no one was listening.

"You and your God seem to have a good thing going, but most of us don't understand it. So, keep it to yourself when we are in public, okay?"

Aaron laughed as he slammed his locker shut. "You think I'm embarrassing? You should see what your hair looks like!"

"Ah, man, I knew it." Trevor grabbed his backpack and ducked into the bathroom across the hall. Still laughing, Aaron moved to his next class.

> *They celebrate your abundant goodness and*
> *joyfully sing of your righteousness.*
> Psalm 145:7

What About You?

Are you willing to tell others that God is the One Who brings good things into your life?

Like...

- The good abilities and talents you have that help you achieve your dreams?
- An answer to a prayer?
- Giving God the credit for something good you see in His creation?

Take Time to Pray

Thank God for His abundant goodness. Then ask God to help you to celebrate His abundant goodness by sharing with a friend one good thing God has done for you.

Day 4
MY GOD IS ACCEPTING

Read: Psalm 6:9

Avery, alone at the dinner table, stared down at her plate covered in creamed corn.

"Creamed corn makes me gag! Do you want me to throw up on the kitchen table?" Avery yelled to her mother, who was reading in the living room.

"Fine," Avery mumbled to herself when she didn't hear a response, "if nobody is listening, then nobody will notice." Taking a spoon, she shoveled the corn into her mouth. With cheeks bulging, she erupted from the table, ran through the living room, and went straight to the bathroom at the end of the hall. Slamming the door behind her, Avery raised the toilet seat and spit the yellow mush into the bowl. As she flushed, she heard a knock at the door.

"Avery, are you okay?" her mom asked.

"Sure, Mom. I finished the corn, and I had to go to the bathroom badly."

The rest of the evening, Avery avoided her mom. By bedtime, she was feeling sick; and she knew it wasn't from the corn. As she knelt beside her bed to pray, Avery found that she was at a loss regarding what she should say to God. She paused for a moment, then began, "Dear God, I'm sure You don't want to listen to me. You probably don't even like me anymore. Don't You understand? I don't like creamed corn! I guess I should have eaten it. This whole corn thing has ruined my evening. Hang on, God, I'll be back in a minute."

Avery got up from her knees, pulled her blonde hair into a ponytail, and went in search of her mother, who was still sitting on the couch, reading.

"Mom, sorry to interrupt, but I didn't eat the corn. I spit it into the toilet."

"I know, Avery. I saw what happened. I am glad you finally came and told me."

"So, how are you going to discipline me?" wondered Avery.

"Well, we'll discuss that tomorrow. Right now, you need to head to bed; and don't forget to talk to God about this."

"Don't worry, Mom, I already did," Avery said over her shoulder as she made her way back to bed.

Returning once again to her knees, Avery finished her prayer. "Okay, God, I feel better. Thanks for listening, even when things are not right. It's great to know You accept me, no matter what, and that You help me make things better. Amen."

The LORD has heard my cry for mercy; the LORD accepts my prayer.
Psalm 6:9

What About You?

Are there times when you feel you have done something that has kept God from accepting you and your prayers?

Like...

- When you are mean to someone at school?
- When you are disobedient or dishonest?
- When you deny your love for God in front of your friends?

Take Time to Pray!

God is faithful to forgive your sins when you confess them and say you are sorry (I John 1:9). Thank God for His forgiveness and let God know how amazing it is that He loves you and is ready to listen to your prayers.

Day 5
MY GOD IS ACTIVE

Read: Hebrews 4:12

Bright sunlight filled Avery's bedroom as she rolled over and squinted up at her window.

"Ugh, I hate when I forget to close the blinds," she groaned as she buried her head under the pillow. But it was no use hiding, and Avery knew it. This morning, the sun was her silent alarm.

"Well, I guess I'm awake, whether I want to be or not; so I might as well do my devotions," Avery mumbled as she struggled to sit up in bed. Once she had her pillows in place, she reached for her Bible and began to read Psalm 147. Following her regular routine, Avery looked for a verse or two that would challenge or encourage her. This morning, she selected verses ten and eleven; and as she read them, she began to laugh. "'His pleasure is not in the strength of the horse, nor his delight in the legs of a warrior; the LORD delights in those who fear him, who put their hope in his unfailing love.'"

Still laughing, Avery set down her Bible and began to talk to God.

"God, You never sleep in—even this morning, You have given me the perfect verses." Avery glanced at her clock and then continued to pray, "In three hours, I'll be up at the stables getting ready to jump Rio for the first time. My hope isn't in Rio or the strength of my own legs. My hope is in You! Oh, and thanks, God, that You are active in every area of my life, including jumping Rio. Thanks that Your Bible always has a word for me!"

Ready for the adventures of the day, Avery jumped out of bed and smiled at the sunshine.

"Get ready, world; with God's help, Rio and I are going to fly!"

For the word of God is alive and active . . .
Hebrews 4:12a

What About You?

One way God is active in your life is by speaking to you through His words that are found in the Bible.

Like . . .

- When you read the verse at the beginning of these devotionals and ask, "What does it mean to me?"

- When you find a verse you need, and you memorize it?

- When a Sunday School teacher reads a story from the Bible, and you listen and learn from it?

Take Time to Pray!

Thank God that He is actively involved in your life. Ask God to help you listen and learn from His words found in the Bible.

Day 6
MY GOD IS ALIVE

Read: Acts 1:1-3

The basketball rolled slowly around the rim as Trevor and Aaron anxiously waited under the hoop.

"Yes! My basket, my game!" Aaron announced as the ball dropped through the net. Aaron celebrated with a victory dance, then challenged his friend to another game. "Come on, Trev, best three out of five?"

"Nah, I should be getting home. My mom will be done her shift soon, and I'm supposed to have the hamburgers sizzled and served before she walks through the door," said Trevor.

Ignoring his friend, Aaron picked up the ball and began to dribble it up and down his driveway.

"Come on and do this drill with me."

Trevor ran his hands over his hair, smoothing it into place. Then, as he bent down to pick up his sweatshirt, he said, "It's not like I want to go home. My mom is so angry these days that I would rather be anywhere else than home, but I have no choice."

Aaron grabbed the ball and held it against one hip.

"Trev, you and your mom need God. He wants to help."

Trevor shook his head in disgust.

"Aaron, I saw a sign the other day. It said, 'God is dead.' And you know what I thought? *What God?* If you ask me, my line on this whole God thing is if you can't see it, then you can't believe it."

Aaron tossed the ball to Trevor, forcing him to drop his sweatshirt.

"Okay, Trev, what about Jesus, God's Son? He was seen by many people. Jesus did die, but He rose again. Jesus is alive!"

Trevor dropped the ball, grabbed his sweatshirt, and walked down the drive. Without looking back, he threw out his final thought, "That's a nice story for Sunday school boys."

After his suffering, [Jesus] presented himself to them and gave many convincing proofs that he was alive...

Acts 1:3a

What About You?

Can you think of ways you can know God is alive?
Like...

- Seeing God's hand in the creation around you?
- Knowing God has heard your prayers and answered them?
- Understanding that the Bible is God's letter to you?

Take Time to Pray!

Thank God that He is real and that Jesus is alive!

Day 7

MY GOD IS ALMIGHTY

Read: Psalm 91:1

Avery, with a sponge in hand, swiped away the water from Rio's neck. The warm fall sun kept Avery comfortable as the cool water ran down her forearm and dripped from her elbow. With the last wipe, she leaned her blonde head against Rio's wet side, and a smile spread across her face.

I did it! I got Rio over the jump—with God's help! Sure, the jump was only a foot off the ground, but we flew over it together!

Sensing her pleasure, Rio lifted his head and nuzzled his owner, his soft muzzle working away at a mouthful of grass. The sound of footsteps on the stones behind Avery drew her attention to James. She turned and smiled up at her coach as he leaned his lanky body against Rio's rump.

"You did it!" James praised Avery.

"I had help," Avery confessed.

"Well, I do what I can as a trainer, but it was you sitting in that saddle."

"James, you are a great trainer." Avery laughed. "But I was talking about God. Just before I went over the jump, I gave my fears to God; and He gave me the strength to make the jump. My dad calls it 'resting in the Almighty.'"

James' brow creased in confusion as he shook his head at his student. "And all this time, I thought my training was the key to your success."

Avery giggled at James as he put on a pout. "Hey, next to God, you are the best trainer a girl could have!"

James smiled his acceptance of the compliment as Avery tugged on Rio's lead rope. Together, they turned toward the barn.

Whoever dwells in the shadow of the Most High will rest in the shadow of the Almighty.
Psalm 91:1

What About You?

You, too, can rest in the shadow of the Almighty.
Like...

- When you are afraid of failing at something new or difficult.
- When you are anxious about a friendship.
- When you are concerned about the future and changes that are coming.

Take Time to Pray!

The best way to rest in the shadow of the Almighty is to take your concerns to Him in prayer. Do this right now!

Day 8
MY GOD IS APPROACHABLE

Read: Ephesians 3:12

It was a cool Monday morning at Glenwood Middle School, and the students were milling about the halls. Avery grabbed her math book from the locker and scurried to Ms. Phillips' class, hoping to have a moment before the rest of the class arrived.

After two sharp knocks on the door, Avery pushed it open and entered her homeroom. "Excuse me, Ms. Phillips, may I talk with you?" Avery asked as she flung her long blonde hair over her shoulder.

Ms. Phillips slowly looked up from her desk, her short hair teased into a puff on top of her head and her glasses perched on the end of her nose.

After a moment of silence, Avery continued, "Chris is moving next Friday. I thought it would be nice to have a going-away party for him. He's been part of our class for the past four years; and anyway . . . well, I mean . . . if I make the cake and some of the kids do the decorating . . . well, could we have a party?"

By the time Avery finished talking, her heart was pounding hard. It didn't help that Ms. Phillips' cold eyes were staring her down.

Finally, Ms. Phillips replied, "I was preparing your homework assignment, Avery. I would call this an unnecessary interruption."

"Please, Ms. Phillips, I'll take care of all the details." Avery waited in silence as her teacher considered the proposal.

"I'll give you ten minutes at the end of next Friday. You must submit a written schedule and party plan. I will not be bothered with any of the details. You are on your own, understand?"

Avery nodded her head vigorously as she turned and left the class.

Trevor leaned against his locker while running his fingers through his messy hair. He noticed Avery's flushed face and called to her, "What have you been up to in Fussy Phillips' class?"

Avery hushed Trevor as she came alongside the lockers. "I got Ms. Phillips to agree to a going-away party for Chris. It will be next Friday at the end of the day. You, Aaron, and Kaylin have to help, okay?"

Trevor raised an eyebrow in shocked disbelief. "Hey, if you had the guts to ask Ms. Phillips, then you deserve all the help we can give you."

> *In him and through faith in him we may approach God with freedom and confidence.*
>
> Ephesians 3:12

What About You?

There are many people on earth you may be nervous to talk to, but you can always approach God with confidence knowing that He wants to hear from you anytime, anywhere, regarding anything.

Like...

- When you ask for help on a test you are taking.
- When you ask for patience when you are waiting for an answer.
- When you ask for direction because you want to make the right choice.

Take Time to Pray!

Talk to God about a concern you have. God wants to hear about what is happening in your life.

Day 9

MY GOD IS MY ATONEMENT

Read: Hebrews 2:17

It took some time to convince Kaylin, but Avery had finally managed to talk her into coming to their youth group at church.

As the girls walked up the church steps, Kaylin asked Avery, "What's the name of this group again?"

"The Bridge," Avery responded.

"Will I know anybody besides Aaron here?"

"Sure, you'll recognize some people from school. You'll like our youth pastor, Steve; he's always thinking up fun things to do," Avery assured her friend.

As soon as the girls entered the youth room, they were each handed a colored button that identified them as part of a team.

A few minutes later, Steve, a short redheaded guy with a big smile, gathered the group of preteens around him. After welcoming them, he gave them the instructions for the game. "Okay, you need to go to the table that has the same colored bowl as the button you were handed when you came in. Set your buttons on the edge of the table, so half of the button is off the edge. Using your thumbnail, flick the button and try to flip it into the bowl. The first person to get his or her button in the bow is your atonement guy or girl. Each of you will have a youth leader at the table counting the number of tries you have before the first button makes it into the bowl."

The groups were formed, and the buttons flew. It wasn't as easy as it looked. Finally, an atonement person was established from each table, and these people were called to the front of the room. Avery represented the red group. She grinned when she saw that Aaron won the position for the yellow group.

Once everyone was seated, Steve explained, "These four winners are our atonement people. Atonement means, 'pays the price.' These lucky four people get to pay the price for the total number of tries it took your team to flick the button in the bowl. And how do they pay the price for all your misses? By doing push-ups into a pile of stinky socks and shoes!"

The "winners" groaned and gagged, while the rest of the kids howled and cheered. Steve finished the instructions over the noise.

"Let's take off your socks and shoes and pile them in front of your atonement winner."

Amid a lot of laughter and groans, the piles were formed; and the push-ups began. Every time the atonement people came near the ground, their noses dipped into the stinky pile. Avery was glad her team's number of tries was so low because she finished first. Glancing across the room, she saw Aaron was still dipping his nose into the stinky pile.

Steve, once again, got the group seated and settled. After socks and shoes were back on the owners' feet, Steve concluded the game by saying, "Christ is our Atonement. We have missed the perfect standard God set when we sinned, just like when you all missed getting the button into the bowl. Someone who could meet the standard had to pay the price. In the game, it was the winner; in our lives, it is Jesus Christ Who had to pay the price for our misses—for our sins. Jesus' death was worse than dipping into stinky socks; He took our sins on Himself through His death on the cross. Jesus paid the price. He died for you and for me. Jesus is our Atonement Guy!"

That he might make atonement for the sins of the people.
Hebrews 2:17b

What About You?

Do you recognize the fact that you have missed God's perfect standard and you need someone to make an atonement—to pay the price—for your sins?

Like...

- When you are mean to a sister or brother—that sin needs to be paid for?

- When you are dishonest with your teacher—that sin means you missed the perfect standard?

- When you have angry thoughts toward your parents—that is called sin?

Take Time to Pray!

Thank Jesus for paying the price for all your misses—your sins. Let Him know you are glad He is your Atonement Guy.

+ Day 10

MY GOD IS ATTENTIVE

Read: I Peter 3:12

Kaylin walked into her high-rise apartment after The Bridge, excited and eager to share the evening's events with her parents. Her parents were both propped up in bed, busy working on their laptops. When Kaylin walked into their bedroom, neither of them bothered to look up.

"Hey, I'm home," ventured Kaylin.

"Did you lock the door?" questioned Kaylin's mom without taking her eyes off her laptop.

"Yep," Kaylin answered as she sat down on the edge of their bed. After a minute or two of silence, Kaylin decided to try again. "Mom, Dad, do you want to hear about my night at the church group?"

Her dad removed his thick-rimmed glasses as he paused for a moment to share his thoughts. "Just as long as they don't put too much 'God talk' into your head, I don't think we need to hear the details."

Without waiting for a response, Kaylin's dad slipped his glasses back into place and went on with his reading.

Kaylin slowly got up from their bed and dragged herself to her own room. She shut the door behind her, flicked on her pink lamp, and settled herself into her swinging chair. In the semi-darkness, she was glad she had a God Who wanted to listen.

"God, this prayer thing is new for me. Let me just say I am glad You are attentive to my prayers; I am glad You like to listen to my words and my thoughts. I know You are here tonight, and I am glad You want to hear about my night."

Kaylin pulled her blue comforter off her bed. Once it was tucked around her, she began to tell God all about her first night at The Bridge.

> *For the eyes of the Lord are on the righteous and his ears are attentive to their prayer...*
> *I Peter 3:12a*

What About You?

God was with Kaylin the entire night while she was at The Bridge, yet He is a God Who still wants to hear her thoughts regarding her evening at church. When you feel no one is listening, do you turn to God and share with Him what is on your heart?

Like...

- When someone embarrasses you at school?
- When you are excited about something great and no one else is?
- When you have questions, and you don't know who to ask?

Take Time to Pray!

What thoughts do you need to share? Share those thoughts right now with God because He is attentive and will listen and care.

Day 11

MY GOD IS AVENGING

Read: Romans 12:19

The sweat ran into Aaron's eyes as he dribbled the ball down the basketball court.

"Pass the ball!" yelled Coach Ryder. "Aaron, pass the ball! This is a team sport, not a one-man show!"

Aaron knew he could make the shot, but he also knew he had better not try. Stalling at the top of the key, he passed the ball to Booker, a tall, skinny eighth grader. As Booker went up for the shot, Aaron was hit from behind. The elbow caught him right in the kidney. Aaron dropped to one knee in agony.

As the rest of the players were busy under the basket, Aaron felt hot breath on the back of his neck. Through the court noise he heard, "That's what we do to show-offs. If you think we're going to let you make this team, guess again!"

Aaron raised his head as Jeremy walked toward the bench on the sideline. Everything inside Aaron wanted to go to the coach and tell him what Jeremy had just done; but Aaron knew he wouldn't look like a team player, and the coach wouldn't like that. Instead, he silently prayed as he went to join the team for the next drill.

God, Jeremy isn't good for the team. I'm so mad at him. I don't think he should be a part of this team, but I'm going to leave that with You.

At the end of the drill, Coach Ryder called the players into center court. Once they were all seated, he said, "I'm not going to make you wait long for my decision regarding who has made the team. Give me ten minutes; and once you are showered and dressed, you will find the list posted outside the gym door."

Ten minutes later, Aaron stepped outside the gym door just in time to see Jeremy whip a basketball across the gym, pick up his gym bag, and storm out the door. Confused by the angry display, Aaron turned to the list taped to the wall. Scanning down to the M's, Aaron's stomach flip-flopped when he saw the name Aaron March.

"Yes! I made it!" yelled Aaron as he turned and strode out of the gym. Stepping into the warm September sunshine, a smile spread across his face as he realized that Jeremy's name was not on the list.

> *Do not take revenge, my dear friends,*
> *but leave room for God's wrath, for it is written:*
> *"It is mine to avenge; I will repay," says the Lord.*
>
> Romans 12:19

What About You?

Do you ever feel like you want to hurt someone who has hurt you—to take your own revenge?

Like...

- When someone lies about you?

- When someone makes fun of you?

- When someone doesn't play fair?

Take Time to Pray!

Ask God to help you forgive the person who has hurt you, then thank God for taking care of the situation in His time and in His way so that you don't have to worry about it.

Day 12
MY GOD IS AWESOME

Read: Psalm 47:1-2

Avery twirled her pen between her fingers as she stared at the classroom clock.
Ten seconds 'til Chris' party starts. How will Ms. Phillips ever finish in time?
As if on cue, Ms. Phillips shut her math book and removed her glasses. "Attention, class, Avery has an announcement to make."
Avery dropped her pen in surprise as she wiggled out of her chair and quickly made her way to the front of the room. Tucking her hair behind one ear, she cleared her throat, trying hard to hide her grin.
"Attention, class," Avery mimicked Ms. Phillips, "I have an announcement to make. We all know that Chris is leaving, and we are very sorry to see him go. But we don't want to spend the last ten minutes with him being sad, so instead, *let's party!*"
As Avery yelled the last words, Aaron cranked up the music on his phone; and the guys in the back row let the streamers fly over the heads of their classmates. With music blaring and streamers flying, Avery called Chris up to the front of the class. Chris' freckled face flushed bright red as Avery displayed a big, white cake ablaze with sparklers, thanks to Kaylin. *We'll Miss You*, written in bright green icing, covered the top of the cake. When the sparklers fizzled out, Avery quickly cut the cake, and Kaylin passed out the pieces. The school bell rang just as the last piece of cake was delivered.
"That signals the end of another school day." Ms. Phillips' voice resonated above the music. "It's time to be on your way with your piece of cake. Oh, and, Chris, all the best at your next school."

Aaron turned off the music as they quickly cleared the classroom. The boys in the back row picked up the streamers. Kaylin crushed the cake box and shoved it in the trash can while Avery thanked Ms. Phillips for the ten-minute party.

Out in the hall, Chris finished his last bite of cake as his friends said goodbye.

When Avery came out of the classroom, Chris was quick to call her over. "Hey, Avery, that was a great ten-minute party. Don't know how you ever got Ms. Phillips to say yes, but that's what makes you so awesome!"

Avery chuckled at Chris. He was so thrilled with the surprise that he hadn't noticed that he had green and white icing stuck to his top lip. "Chris, it's God Who is awesome—I just have fun helping Him make people happy."

For the LORD Most High is awesome,
the great King over all the earth.

Psalm 47:2

What About You?

Are there times when you are quick to praise others, but you forget to praise God?

Like...

- When your parents give you an unexpected surprise?

- When you get an invitation to an event you really want to attend?

- When you have the opportunity to earn some extra money?

Take Time to Pray!

God likes to hear He is awesome. Choose one thing God has done for you and tell Him how awesome He is for doing it!

Day 13

MY GOD IS BEAUTIFUL

Read: Psalm 27:4

The doors of the aquarium swung open as Glenwood students rushed indoors. The students, glad to get out of the pouring rain, jostled each other, eager to experience the underwater world.

Aaron and Trevor gave each other a high five when it was announced that they were in the same group of guys. The two boys had one thought; and they quickly shared it with Mrs. McCinty, the parent volunteer for their group.

"The sharks!" Aaron announced.

"Yeah, the sharks!" Trevor chimed in.

Mrs. McCinty smiled at the boys' enthusiasm as she responded with a plan. "Feeding time for the sharks is at 10:00 a.m. That would be the best time to see them in action. So let's visit the coral reef section for the next hour. That will give us ten minutes to be seated and ready for the shark feeding frenzy."

The group all agreed, and off they went to see the under-water wonders.

Mrs. McCinty held open the door as each boy entered the Coral Reef Cave. The space was dark, cool, and damp, with a tank that encased the walls and ceiling. The boys were silent, fascinated with the multi-colored fish that surrounded them. Mrs. McCinty, trying to capture the moment, announced, "Why don't each of you choose the most beautiful fish and share your choice with the group?"

"Ugh!"

"Forget it!"

"Oh, look at this dead one with its guts hanging out!"

These comments all came at once from random boys. Mrs. McCinty knew she had lost, so she let the boys enjoy the beauty in their own way.

Aaron removed himself from the rest of the group while imagining what it would be like to discover such beauty on his own, in the wide-open ocean. He laughed at the black and yellow-striped guy with a pig-like nose, and he wondered if the checkerboard fish liked to play games. He tried, without success, to follow the florescent purple fish that darted between the yellow and pink coral.

As the noise from the rest of the guys faded into the background, Aaron stood in his own space, lost in his own thoughts, wondering about the beauty of God Who created such beautiful things.

> *One thing I ask from the LORD, this only do I seek ... to gaze on the beauty of the LORD and to seek him in his temple.*
>
> *Psalm 27:4*

What About You?

What is the most beautiful thing you have seen in God's creation?

Like ...

- Exotic flowers?
- A bright green lizard?
- A brilliant sunset?

Take Time to Pray!

Thank God that He has chosen to reveal His beauty in the creation we see around us.

Day 14

MY GOD IS BLAMELESS

Read: Psalm 18:25

The fall breeze blew past Aaron as he waited patiently on Trevor's front porch. Through the screen door, he could see Trevor bouncing the soccer ball from knee to knee.

"Come on!" called Aaron. "We can't start the game without the ball. Everyone is waiting for us."

"Forty-one, forty-two, forty-three . . . I can't stop now . . . forty-four . . . I'm close to a personal best," Trevor panted.

Aaron leaned against the screen, wondering what magic number was Trevor's personal best. Suddenly, Aaron noticed Trevor was getting dangerously close to the coffee table.

"Hey, Trev, watch out!" But Aaron's warning came too late. Trevor fell backward over the coffee table and sent the glass vase smashing against the living room wall. Aaron threw open the screen door and ran to Trevor.

"Are you okay?" Aaron asked as he looked down at Trevor on his back sprawled across the coffee table.

"Oh, man, am I in trouble," Trevor moaned. "My mom is forever saying not to play soccer inside. So much for my personal best! When my mom gets home, that'll be my personal worst."

Aaron looked over at the tiny pieces sprayed across the moss-green carpet. He was at a loss for words.

"Man." Trevor groaned as he rolled off the table and began to pace the room. "Why do things like this always happen to me? If your God is so perfect, why didn't He stop me? He didn't have to let this happen. It's all your God's fault!"

"Hey, don't blame God for your mistakes," Aaron insisted. "Listen, I'd stay and help you put the pieces back together if I thought it would help; but the guys are waiting, so can I have the ball?"

Trevor grunted, "Yeah, have fun. Don't think about how my life will end within the hour when my mom gets home from work."

Aaron grabbed the ball and shrugged his shoulders as he pushed open the screen door. With a shake of his head, he thought to himself, *This could have been avoided if Trev had just obeyed his mom's rule.*

> *To the blameless you show yourself blameless.*
> Psalm 18:25b

What About You?

Have you ever done something wrong and found yourself quick to blame God for your mistake?

Like...

- When you disobey and get caught?
- When you break something and get blamed?
- When you are selfish, and it backfires?

Take Time to Pray!

Say sorry to God for the times when you have blamed Him for your mistakes, then make a commitment to God that you will not blame Him when things go wrong.

+ Day 15

MY GOD IS A BLESSING

Read: Ezekiel 34:26

The gray day appeared to hold no hope for Kaylin as she leaned against the windowpane and watched the rain pelt against the glass. Late last night, Kaylin's parents announced that they would need to work all day Saturday. As a result, a lonely Saturday stretched before her. Kaylin, busy feeling sorry for herself, sighed as her phone buzzed.

"Hi, Christi," Kaylin enthused to her favorite next-door neighbor.

"Hi, Kaylin, sorry to call last minute, but McCall needs some help with a school project, and I am wondering if you want to earn a little extra money by giving her a hand?"

"Sounds great!" Kaylin responded. "I'll be right over."

Kaylin carefully locked her apartment door, then she padded down the hallway of their high-rise apartment building to her nearest neighbor. McCall opened the door just as Kaylin went to raise the knocker.

"Kaylin, this is so cool. I have so much to do, and my mom is too busy with her work project to help." McCall, a seven-year-old with blond curls, bounced her way into the dining room where the school project waited.

The rest of the day flew by for Kaylin. Her projects involved baking cookies, decorating a poster, and creating a log cabin made from popsicle sticks. Kaylin enjoyed every minute working with McCall and being creative. Their time was pleasantly interrupted with a macaroni and cheese lunch and afternoon snacks of popcorn and a caramel apple. As the clock chimed 4:00, McCall set the last popsicle stick into place. Kaylin crossed the living room and called upstairs to Christi, who was working in her office space on the upper landing.

"Christi, do you have a minute to look at our finished product?"

"I have more than a minute," Christi announced as she made her way down the spiral staircase. "Kaylin, because of all your help, I was able to email the final draft to my boss. So let me look at your final product, and then we can go for a swim and soak in the hot tub in our indoor pool downstairs."

"Woohoo!" cheered McCall from the dining room.

"And this," whispered Christi as she slipped fifty dollars into Kaylin's hand, "is to say thank you."

Kaylin grinned as Christi went ahead of her into the dining room.

Thank You, God! You know I need this money for Christmas. You have turned a lonely day into an awesome day!

> *I will send down showers in season;*
> *there will be showers of blessing.*
>
> Ezekiel 34:26b

What About You?

Do you look for God's blessings throughout your day? Like . . .

- When you wake up to another day to live life?

- When you sit down for dinner and enjoy a selection of good food?

- When you go to bed at night in a home where you have a bed and a roof over your head?

Take Time to Pray!

Look back over your day. Choose one blessing God gave you and thank Him for His goodness.

Day 16
MY GOD IS THE BREAD OF LIFE

Read: John 6:35

The March family took a tight corner as they pulled out of the church parking lot. Aaron, who was slumped in the corner of the back seat, wished he were anywhere else but sitting beside his younger brother.

"Mom, Aaron is putting his foot on my side," lied Justin.

"Ah, Mom, I'm not doing anything back here. I'm just minding my own business," defended Aaron.

"Boys, I need both of you to sit still until we get home. My special homemade bread has been rising all morning, and the soup is ready to be reheated. It will not take long for lunch to be on the table. I'm hoping a little food will change both of your moods," stated his mom from the front seat.

Justin leaned forward between the front seats, confused by something. "Mom, in communion this morning, the pastor said something about Jesus being the Bread of Life. He said if we come to Jesus, we will never be hungry. So why am I hungry for lunch?"

Aaron groaned as he stuck out his foot and pushed his seven-year-old brother to the far side of the car. "Stupid, the Bible isn't talking about physical hunger; it's talking about spiritual hunger."

"Mom, Aaron called me stupid," Justin whined.

"Aaron," their father said from behind the wheel, "we don't say stupid. It is a smart question and a smart answer from you, too, Aaron. Your brother is correct, Justin. When you say thank You to Jesus for dying for you on the cross, He gives you eternal life. You get to spend forever in Heaven with him. But that's not all. You will find, here on earth, that God is the Answer to all your wants and needs, He satisfies your spiritual hunger. We have an opportunity to thank God for satisfying our spiritual hunger as we remember Jesus' death and resurrection through communion. Does that mean that because I have said thank You to Jesus for what He did for us by dying on the cross, I shouldn't want any more of your mom's homemade bread for lunch?"

Aaron grunted to himself as he looked out the window at the passing cars.

"Think about it, Justin. Dad lets God satisfy his spiritual hunger, and he gets to have homemade bread for lunch, too. That's the good thing about following God."

> Then Jesus declared, "I am the bread of life.
> Whoever comes to me will never go hungry,
> and whoever believes in me will never be thirsty."
> John 6:35

What About You?

Do you ever find yourself hungry for something besides food? Like . . .

- Excitement?
- Time alone to do your own thing?
- Attention from a parent or friend?

Take Time to Pray!

We all need to recognize that we have been created with a hunger for God. Thank God for the friendship He provides that can satisfy your hunger for good things and for more of God.

Day 17
MY GOD IS THE BREATH OF LIFE

Read: Job 33:4

As soon as Avery got home from church, she pulled on her riding gear.

"Hurry, Mom, I need to be at the barn by 1:00," called Avery as she opened the back door. "I'm out in the garage putting on my boots. Will you bring my sandwich with you?"

"Be there in a minute," her mom responded from the kitchen.

Avery pulled her riding boots over her beige riding pants; then she smoothed her black sweater as she straightened. With her blonde hair pulled back in a ponytail and helmet tucked under her arm, she was the perfect picture of an English horseback rider.

Avery and her mom slipped into the front seat of the car, and they were soon on their way to the barn. In the car, Avery finished her sandwich. After a moment's silence, she decided to share her mixed emotions concerning her jumping lesson.

"Mom, you know that I think that Rio is ready to go over the two-foot jump, but I'm just not sure *I'm* ready. I want to try it, but I'm afraid I will fall off. I'm just not sure." Avery shared these last few words as her mother pulled in front of the barn.

"Go for it, Avery, and give your fears over to God. I'll look forward to hearing all about the jump when I pick you up at 4:00," encouraged her mother as Avery jumped out of the car.

Within the hour, Avery had Rio warmed up and ready to try some serious jumping.

James, Avery's riding trainer, stood in the center of the outdoor ring, giving Avery a few last-minute instructions.

"Avery, remember to give Rio a lot of leg as you approach the jump," he instructed as she began the round.

Avery kept Rio at a canter as she took the corner and approached the first jump. Her heart was pounding as she squeezed her calves tightly just in front of the jump. Avery, not ready for Rio's refusal, went flying over her horse's head and the jump. She landed with a thud on the other side.

James rushed over to see if Avery was okay. Struggling for breath, Avery grimaced as he checked her for any injuries.

"It looks like you're okay, kid. You just got the wind knocked out of you. Come on, let's get you on your feet and back in the saddle." James helped Avery struggle to her feet. Once back on Rio, Avery began again. It took her five more tries, but she finally got Rio over the jump.

That night, Avery knelt beside her bed to say her prayers.

"God, thanks for every breath You give me. They come so easily . . . they are a gift from you. When I was lying on the other side of the jump, I was frightened. Without my breath, I have no life. Thanks for the life You have given me and for helping me get over that jump. Amen."

The Spirit of God has made me;
the breath of the Almighty gives me life.

Job 33:4

What About You?

Have you ever thought about how precious each breath is? Like . . .

- When you are swimming underwater?
- When you are blowing up a balloon?
- When you have had the wind knocked out of you?

Take Time to Pray!

Thank God for giving you each breath and for being the Breath of Life.

Day 18

MY GOD IS BRILLIANT

Read: Ezekiel 1:25-28

It was Wednesday afternoon, and the storm that had been raging all day had finally blown past as the school bell signaled the end of another school day. Trevor and Aaron were the first two students out of Glenwood's front door.

"No homework, Trev! This is a perfect chance to check out the new construction site on Bell Line Road," suggested Aaron.

"Yeah, let's do it. Let's see what kind of cool stuff we can find lying around," agreed Trevor as he jumped the puddle in his path.

The two guys discussed their great construction site finds from past years as they walked down Glenwood Avenue. Stopping at the convenience store, they each bought a bag of chips. Then, crossing the road, the two decided to take a shortcut through the woods so they could pick up Bell Line Road on the other side. They were just shoving the empty chip bags into their pockets when they emerged from the woods into a large field, the final barrier between them and Bell Line.

"I never thought about how the rain would wreck this field. It's a swamp!" declared Trevor.

"Looks like we have two choices; swim it or walk around it," groaned Aaron.

As the two boys stood side-by-side considering their options, the clouds parted, and the sun broke through. They watched as a rainbow appeared in the sky.

"Wow, out of nowhere. I've never seen one so bright and clear," said Trevor.

"My brilliant God makes brilliant things!" stated Aaron with a cheesy smile.

*Brilliant light surrounded him.
Like the appearance of a rainbow in the clouds on a rainy day,
so was the radiance around him . . .*
Ezekiel 1:27b-28a

What About You?

Have you taken the time to notice that your brilliant God makes brilliant things?

Like . . .

- The big dipper formed by stars in the sky?
- The firefly flashing on a warm summer's evenings?
- The sun on a hot summer's day?

Take Time to Pray!

Thank God for being a brilliant God Who makes brilliant things.

+ **Day 19**

MY GOD IS THE BUILDER

Read: Hebrews 3:4

Trevor and Aaron had great hopes of making it to the construction site before dusk, so they decided to walk around the swamp that lay in their path. As the guys crossed Bell Line, the sound of a lone hammer tapping out its uneven rhythm reverberated over the traffic noise that was fading into the distance.

"Ah, man, someone is still working at the site," complained Trevor as he picked up a stone and threw it at a road sign.

"Maybe he won't mind if we look around," hoped Aaron optimistically. The two carefully stepped over the wood planks stacked in small piles in front of the framed house. The hammering, now strong and steady, made them wonder if they would be able to catch the worker's attention to ask permission to look around.

"Errr, hello," yelled Aaron. "Excuse me, sir!" The hammering stopped as a thin man with a tan face and gray eyes turned and smiled at the boys beneath him. "We hate to interrupt your hard work, but we would love to look around if that's okay with you?"

Before the man could answer, Trevor chimed in, "Hey, why are you here all alone?"

The man swung down from the beam on which he had been balancing, slipped the hammer into his toolbelt, and ran his fingers through his hair.

"Well, boys, I'm the builder, the creator of this place. I can see my dream becoming a reality. When the rain started to pour, there was little my workers could do; so, I sent them home. For me . . . well, there is always something to do."

"Wow, will this be your place when you're done?" Trevor wondered.

"I'll share it with others," the man said, "although I'm sure no one will love it as much as I do."

"Do you mind if we look around?" asked Aaron politely.

"Let me do even better, how about a tour?"

"Yeah! Sure!" the two guys chimed in response.

The next hour flew by as the builder shared his plans and dreams about the house. Aaron found a twisted tool he was allowed to keep, and Trevor gathered stone chips with a metallic sheen and an oddly bent nail that he would add to his collection.

The setting sun signaled dinnertime, and so the two guys thanked the builder for his time and attention.

As they made their way down Bell Line, Trevor wondered aloud, "Do you think every builder is as proud of his creation as that guy was?"

Aaron smiled to himself, even as he thought, *I know One Builder Who is!*

For every house is built by someone, but God is the builder of everything.

Hebrews 3:4

What About You?

God is proud of what He has created and that includes you. What do you feel He did best when He made you?

Like . . .

- Your smile?

- Your athletic ability?

- Your brain?

Take Time to Pray!

Thank God for the great way He built you. Ask Him to continue to build you into the godly person He wants you to be.

Day 20

MY GOD IS CALLING

Read: II Thessalonians 1:11

Kaylin's new shoe caught on the car door, sending her and her purse sprawling across the shopping mall sidewalk. Avery emerged from the car as Kaylin swiped her stuff back into her purse, rubbed her knee, then got back on her feet.

"My mom says these heels are too high, but I don't care. I love them!" Kaylin insisted.

Avery stifled a giggle as she went to shut the door.

"Pick us up in an hour, okay, Mom?"

A short honk was her answer as her mother drove away.

"Let's go to Dingle Dangle first. I want to get a new pair of earrings for Friday night's football game," Kaylin suggested as she flung open the mall door.

The walls of the small shop were lined with every accessory imaginable, but it didn't take long for Avery to find the hairclip she wanted to buy. Eager to show it to Kaylin, Avery wound her way to the back of the shop. Just before she reached Kaylin, Avery froze, her eyes fastened on a package peeking out of Kaylin's back pocket. Horrified, Avery grabbed Kaylin's arm and pulled her close.

"Kaylin, I can see the edge of that earring package sticking out of your back pocket. What are you doing—stealing?"

Kaylin's face went bright red as she fumbled a response. "I only have enough money for one pair of earrings, but I found two pairs I just love."

"God has called you to make better choices than that, Kaylin. How do you think He feels sitting up in Heaven watching you steal?" questioned Avery.

"Honestly, God wasn't really on my mind," confessed Kaylin as she dropped her head in embarrassment.

Avery reached behind her friend, pulled out the hidden pair of earrings, and flung them into her basket.

"Come on, let's buy these, then get out of here before you get us both into trouble," Avery urged. "I'll buy this pair of earrings for you, as long as you commit to listening to what God is calling you to do."

*With this in mind, we constantly pray for you,
that our God may make you worthy of his calling . . .*
II Thessalonians 1:11a

What About You?

Is everything you think, say, and do each day worthy of God's calling? Like . . .

- When you are tempted to tell a white lie to keep from getting in trouble?

- When you want to respond with an angry word to a brother or sister who is being mean?

- When you sneak an extra serving of dessert without getting permission?

Take Time to Pray!

Right now, ask God to make you worthy of His calling. Then, each time you are tempted to do something wrong, ask for God's help to make the right choice.

Day 21
MY GOD IS CARING

Read: I Peter 5:7

The marching band was almost through performing as Avery and Kaylin shuffled into an open spot in the football stands. Hoping to be heard, Kaylin yelled into Avery's ear, "At least we got here before the game began. I was so worried we'd be late!"

"I knew we'd make it, and we even managed to get seats on the fifty-yard line," Avery yelled back just as the band finished their song.

The band left the field while Kaylin glanced around hoping to see some other friends. But her smile was replaced with a scowl.

"Avery, those girls are looking at me. I think it's the earrings; they don't match my jacket, do they? What was I thinking?"

"I don't want to get into the earring thing again," grumbled Avery. "What happened at Dingle Dangle is forgiven and forgotten, and I don't want to think about it anymore."

Kaylin gasped in response as she wildly glanced around, hoping nobody heard Avery's comment.

"Don't say that so loudly. I'm still having trouble sleeping at night, worrying that somebody might report me for trying to steal. If that happens, I will never be allowed in Dingle Dangle again."

Avery pushed her friend away, then stared hard into Kaylin's worried eyes. After a long moment, Avery sternly said, "Worrying is a sin! Have you asked God to forgive you for wanting to steal?"

"Yes," whispered Kaylin.

"Then you are forgiven. God has forgotten about it. Just don't do it again. Hey, worrying is not part of God's plan for us. Besides, look how He cares for us—you got your earrings without paying! I had enough money to treat because my dad doubled my allowance; we have good seats at the game; and you look cute in your jacket and new earrings. So, forget your worries and enjoy the game!" Avery managed to get in her last words as the home team charged onto the field and the crowd began to cheer.

Cast all your anxiety on him because he cares for you.
I Peter 5:7

What About You?
Do you spend time worrying?
Like...

- Wondering if you are going to make the team?

- Being nervous that a teacher will hold a past mistake against you?

- Worrying over a text message that left you feeling sad?

Take Time to Pray!
Give your worries to God right now. He cares about the big and little things in your life.

Day 22

MY GOD IS COMPASSIONATE

Read: Joel 2:13

The computer screen gave an eerie glow to Aaron's dark bedroom. A *Student Hard at Work* sign hung from his door handle, securing his solitude. Aaron had spent the last hour on the internet trying to find information for his science project on tendons and tissues. He finally had enough information for his project, and it was time for a break.

Flopping back in his chair, Aaron heaved a sigh of relief. Tired and ready for something new, Aaron swiped his finger across his computer screen and began to scroll. There was a website he wanted to visit; it had popped up unexpectedly while he was doing his research for class. Shifting uneasily in his seat, he glanced over his shoulder, making sure his door was tightly closed; then he clicked.

The next two minutes took Aaron to a site he shouldn't visit—looking at pictures he shouldn't see. Finally, the guilt was too much; and with what little self-control he had left, he clicked out of the site and turned off his computer. In the darkness, Aaron began pacing between his desk and bed, struggling with the images swimming in his mind.

The deep voice of Aaron's dad boomed through Aaron's door, causing him to jump. "Hey, son, are you ready for a break?" Aaron called from the other side of the room.

"Ah, yeah, Dad, just a sec."

He made some noises that sounded like he was getting up from his desk; then he moved to open the door. Aaron stepped into the hall, letting his gaze drop to the floor. As Aaron's dad began to talk, Aaron felt his face grow hot; and he wondered if his dad knew what he had just done.

"We're scooping some ice cream in the kitchen. Do you want a bowl?"

"Sure, I guess so," Aaron half-heartedly responded.

"Boy, you've been spending way too much time in front of the computer if you can't get excited about ice cream." Aaron's dad rubbed his son's head, then turned toward the kitchen.

"Join me at the table if you decide to take me up on my offer," his dad encouraged as he disappeared around the corner. Aaron leaned against the doorframe and rubbed his stomach. He was too upset to eat ice cream. He wondered if God would be compassionate enough to forgive him for visiting a site he shouldn't have seen.

> *Return to the LORD your God, for he is gracious and compassionate, slow to anger and abounding in love, and he relents from sending calamity.*
>
> *Joel 2:13b*

What About You?

We all do things that are wrong; then afterward, we hope nobody discovers our sin. When you struggle inside because you know you are hiding an unconfessed sin, do you recognize the struggle as guilt?

Like...

- Feeling worried that somebody will ask you about what you have done wrong?

- Avoiding people who might know what you have done wrong?

- Getting angry over little things because you are struggling with guilt?

Take Time to Pray!

Ask God to help you recognize those emotions inside you that signal the need to talk to our compassionate God. God wants you to say you are sorry for what you have done wrong.

Day 23

MY GOD IS COMPELLING

Read: II Corinthians 5:14-15

The following day was Friday, and Aaron felt sick the entire day because of his experience on the internet the night before. He was silent through dinner; then with no enthusiasm, he shrugged on his jacket and told his dad he was ready to go to The Bridge.

At The Bridge, the games were fun; and Steve was especially funny during his Bible talk. But Aaron never cracked a smile the whole night.

As the rest of the church youth group enjoyed the doughnuts, Aaron half-heartedly grabbed a chocolate-covered one, then slowly made his way to the front door where his dad would be waiting.

From behind, Aaron heard Steve's voice and turned to see what he wanted.

"Hey, you with the runaway doughnut, wait up!" Steve called with a grin.

Aaron tried to return the smile, but he found he couldn't even look Steve in the eyes.

"Aaron, is something up? I noticed I couldn't get a laugh out of you tonight, not even at my best jokes."

"Ah, I'm just not feeling well."

"In your gut or in your heart?" Steve asked.

Aaron looked up in surprise. How could Steve know? Did he dare share his secret with Steve? Aaron kicked at the carpet as he struggled with knowing what to do. Steve just waited in silence until Aaron was ready to talk.

"Steve," Aaron began haltingly, "do you spend a lot of time on the internet?"

"Yeah, where do you think I get all my great jokes?"

Aaron wondered if Steve was joking now; but he saw sincere eyes staring back at him, so he decided to continue.

"Well, last night, I was working on a school project; and, well, I decided to check out some other sites I know I am not allowed to see, and, well . . . "

"You saw some things you know you shouldn't be looking at." Steve finished Aaron's sentence.

Looking away, Aaron mumbled, "Yeah."

Steve reached out and gave Aaron's shoulder a squeeze.

"Boy, Satan can sure get our curiosity going and make sin look interesting. He never lets us in on the sickness we will feel after we have done something wrong."

"If I could, I would give anything to go back to last night and make the decision not to click on that website," Aaron confessed.

"That's good, Aaron. Remember that the next time Satan tempts you. But for now, I think you need to have a good, long talk with your Heavenly Father. Let Him know how sorry you are and ask Him to take away the pictures that are still in your mind. It might be a long time before those pictures begin to fade, but continue to ask God for His help."

With Steve's last words, Aaron noticed his dad's car pulling up in front of the church.

"I've got to go. Thanks, Steve." Aaron turned away from Steve, hanging his head as he walked toward the door.

Steve needed to say one more thing, so he called out to Aaron just before he got to his dad's car.

"Aaron, thanks for sharing this with me. You know your earthly father needs you to talk to him about this, too. Maybe you can talk with him on the way home."

Although that thought made Aaron feel nervous, he knew God was compelling him to talk to his dad.

For Christ's love compels us . . .
II Corinthians 5:14a

What About You?

Have you noticed that God compels or prompts you to do the right thing, even when it is difficult?

Like . . .

- Telling a parent about a poor grade?

- Realizing that even though everybody else is doing it, it is till wrong to do?

- Asking a trusted adult for help when you need to make better decisions?

Take Time to Pray!

Satan tempts us to do wrong, but God compels us to make it right. Ask God to help you to be sensitive to Him as He compels you to make good choices.

Day 24
MY GOD IS CONCERNED

Read: II Kings 13:23

"How was The Bridge tonight?" Aaron's dad asked as Aaron slipped into the front seat and closed the car door.

"Okay, I guess," Aaron mumbled, shifting uncomfortably in his seat as his dad pulled out of the church parking lot.

Aaron's dad decided to investigate Aaron's somber mood. "The last twenty-four hours, you've been kind of quiet. Is there something wrong?"

"Ummm... well... yeah, I guess there's something."

"Do you want to talk about it?"

"Do I *want* to?" Aaron snorted. "No, I don't *want* to, but I think I *have* to. Steve says I should." Aaron paused for a moment to gather some courage before he continued. "Dad, I think you're going to be mad. Let me just say that I know what I did was wrong. I feel terrible, and I hope it never happens again."

Mr. March raised his eyebrows. "Wow, I think I better hear what the crime was."

"The crime? Well, you know I was on the internet last night."

"Yeah, working on your school project."

"Uh, well, that wasn't all I did. You see, I took a break, and... well ... I went to a site I shouldn't have."

"And you saw things you shouldn't be looking at?" Aaron's dad questioned.

"Yeah," Aaron said simply.

"Oh, that's a tough one, Aaron. Satan makes those sites look very interesting. We figure a little peek won't hurt, but it does." Aaron's dad thought for a moment and then continued, "When you were alone last night looking at that website, were you really alone?"

"I see your point. You mean God was there, don't you?"

"Son, you are never alone when it comes to sin. Satan is there tempting you, but God is also there wanting to help you. What should you have done differently?"

Aaron thought for a moment. "I should have stopped and asked God for strength to say no to visiting that website. Then I should have walked away and gotten some ice cream."

Aaron's dad laughed. "You had to include that part about the ice cream, didn't you?"

Aaron genuinely smiled for the first time that day. "Thanks, Dad, for not yelling at me."

"Thank you for talking to me about it. We'll look into putting a filter on the internet; maybe that will help keep some of the temptations away. You know this won't be the last time Satan will try to tempt you with this, but now you know how to deal with it."

Aaron's dad drove the car into their driveway and turned it off. Aaron went to get out, but his dad had one more thing to say. "You know, Aaron, it's not just me that's concerned about you making good choices; God is concerned for you, too. He wants the very best for you, and He knows that involves wise choices."

"I know, Dad. God and I will have a long talk about all of this tonight."

"Sounds great! Now, are you up for some ice cream?"

Aaron's face lit up. "Ice cream is your answer to all of life's challenges, isn't it, Dad?"

> *But the LORD was gracious to them*
> *and had compassion and showed concern for them . . .*
>
> *II Kings 13:23a*

What About You?

Know that God is by your side all the time. He is concerned that you always make good choices.

Like...

- Choosing to tell the truth, even when it might get you in trouble.

- Choosing to say no to something wrong, even when it looks like fun.

- Choosing to walk away from a situation, even when it embarrasses you.

Take Time to Pray!

Thank God for His concern for you. Ask God to help you in an area where Satan can easily tempt you to make poor choices.

Day 25

MY GOD IS MY CONQUEROR

Read: Romans 8:35-37

A crispy fry fell into Trevor's applesauce just as he shoved the last bite of hotdog into his mouth.

"Eww, that's gross," Trevor mumbled as he and Aaron searched for the culprit. Most of the lunchroom was oblivious to their trouble, but two giggling girls at the next table looked very suspicious.

"Are you enjoying your fries?" Aaron asked Avery and Kaylin.

"Yeah, although we're missing one. Have you seen it?" Avery laughed.

Aaron pushed back his chair and propped one foot on the seat while trying to look tough. "Yeah, girl, and you better get over here and get it before I make you sorry you threw that fry in our direction."

Pretending to be angry, Avery called back, "Hey, that tough black boy act won't work with me!"

Aaron went to reach for the applesauce-covered fry just as the bony hand of Ms. Phillips grabbed his wrist.

"I think this has gone far enough!" Ms. Phillips declared.

Trevor, trying to be funny, chimed in, "Do you mean the flying French fry or the fact that Aaron is trying to act tough?"

"You just crossed the line, young man. If you four can't get along racially, then you won't be getting along at all!" Ms. Phillips steamed. "Now, gather your books and march yourselves down to the principal's office."

The four friends stared after Ms. Phillips as she stormed out of the lunchroom.

Aaron dropped into his chair, shaking his head in disgust. "Oh great, Fussy Phillips will make real trouble out of this. We're going down."

Kaylin, who had been silent through the whole episode, spoke up, "Doesn't Ms. Phillips know that the color of our skin or the slant of our eyes isn't an issue for us? We're friends who love our differences. Doesn't she get that?"

"Obviously not," Trevor said with a moan.

The four friends began to gather up their books along with the remains of their lunch, each fearing the trouble they were facing.

As they walked through the lunchroom door, Trevor shared his thoughts. "I feel like we're going into the ring. I sure wish we had an all-star wrestler who could fight this one for us."

Dropping back beside Avery, Aaron mumbled, "The only way we're going to win is through *Him*!" Aaron's eyes looked toward Heaven as Avery began to pray silently.

> *No, in all these things we are more than*
> *conquerors through him who loved us.*
>
> Romans 8:37

What About You?

Do you ever feel like you are going into the wrestler's ring or onto the battlefield?

Like...

- When you need to ask a grumpy brother or sister for a favor?

- When you are innocent but the whole class is in trouble, and you must go home and tell your parents what happened?

- When your friends are in the middle of a big fight?

Take Time to Pray!

Remember, God is your Conqueror. Ask Him to go ahead of you into the battle zone. Ask God to help you remember to turn to Him whenever you are facing a difficult battle. He is there to help.

Day 26

MY GOD IS CONSISTENT

Read: Malachi 3:6

The four friends found seats in the principal's office while they listened to Ms. Phillips' rant concerning prejudice. She ended her speech to Mr. Davis with the declaration that Glenwood should be consistent in their dealings with prejudiced attitudes and that all four students should be suspended.

Avery gasped as Mr. Davis pushed back from his desk and wiped his round, bald head with a tissue.

"Ms. Phillips," Mr. Davis boomed, "I believe the best course of action would be to call the parents. I will make the phone calls to see who is available for an after-school conference."

Ms. Phillips, somewhat satisfied, grunted as she turned and left the office.

Ten minutes later, the phone calls were made. Avery's mom and Aaron's dad were the only two parents free for an after-school meeting. The four friends shuffled out of Mr. Davis' office feeling rather ill.

"How's God going to handle our trouble this time?" questioned Kaylin, as they walked down the deserted hall to their lockers.

Trevor grumbled to himself; Avery shrugged; but Kaylin's question started Aaron thinking.

"This time?" Aaron questioned. "God handles our troubles the same way every time because He never changes. Romans 8:28 says, 'We know that in all things God works for the good of those who love him, who have been called according to his purpose.'"

"Oh, great, that leaves me out, then, because you know I am not into this 'God stuff' the same way you three are," said Trevor as he slammed his locker shut.

"Hey, we'll pray and just trust that God will work this out for good, just like He always does," suggested Aaron as the four finished at their lockers and headed for their class.

I the LORD do not change...
Malachi 3:6a

What About You?

Have you ever noticed that when "God works for good," it can sometimes be difficult at the beginning but good in the end?

Like...

- When you are grounded for the weekend, but you learn the importance of respecting your parents, and your bedroom gets cleaned?

- When you are innocent, and once your parents discover that, they trust you even more?

- When you are angry at someone at school, but once you talk it through, you become better friends?

Take Time to Pray!

Ask God to help you to trust His consistency and remember that He never changes. God will always work things out for a good purpose when you love God and live like you love Him.

Day 27
MY GOD IS CONVICTING

Read: John 16:8

After school, all four friends were back in Mr. Davis' office ready to watch what God was going to do. Mrs. McPherson and Mr. March were seated with Ms. Phillips standing at attention near the office door.

"Ms. Phillips, would you please close the door and join the group? I think it would be best to hear the children's side of the story first, and then you can share your conclusions," explained the principal.

The four friends stared at each other, wondering which one of them should be the first to speak.

Avery straightened and cleared her throat. "Well, I guess I'm the best one to retell the story." She quickly reviewed the chain of events, including the flying fry and Aaron's pretend tough act. Avery concluded her story with her honest feelings. "I teased Aaron about his 'tough black boy act,' but that was just in fun. I'm glad Aaron is black; he wouldn't be Aaron if he was any other color."

Looking at her friends, Avery spoke for all of them. "Look at us: Kaylin's Asian; Aaron's Afro-American; I have freckles and white skin; and Trevor . . . well, Trevor's tall and skinny, and his hair is usually a mess. But we're still all great friends—despite our differences."

The other three agreed as Mr. Davis turned to Ms. Phillips. "What are your conclusions, Ms. Phillips?"

Ms. Phillips' face softened as she looked at the four students and then turned to the two parents.

"My conclusion is that I have wasted your time. I mistook Avery's tone and intentions, and I missed Trevor's attempt at humor. I can see now that these four students actually set a wonderful example for the other students. I wish all our students would celebrate their differences."

Mr. March stood up, signaling the end of their meeting. The rest stood as Mr. March shook Ms. Phillips' hand. "I like your desire to eliminate prejudiced attitudes, and I wish it were practiced inside and outside of Glenwood!"

They all agreed as they left Mr. Davis' office.

As the group walked toward the front doors, Avery announced, "God came through again. I think we just witnessed a miracle. Not only did Ms. Phillips get convicted about her wrong conclusions, but she also admitted she was wrong!"

Everybody laughed.

And when he comes, he will convict the world of its sin, and of God's righteousness, and the coming judgment.
John 16:8 (NLT)

What About You?

Have you ever recognized that God was convicting you of sin in your life? Are you willing to admit you are wrong like Ms. Phillips did? Like...

- Forgetting to give back to God some of the money He has given to you? When you give that money to God, that's called tithing.

- Speaking disrespectfully to your parents?

- Expressing your anger with your friends or on the sports field?

Take Time to Pray!

Ask God to convict you of sin in your life. Spend a minute in silence and wait for the Lord to bring a sin to your mind. Say *sorry* for that sin and then ask Him to help you not to do the same sin over again.

Day 28

MY GOD IS THE CORNERSTONE

Read: Ephesians 2:20

The new art museum loomed ahead of Avery and Kaylin as they strode down the sidewalk.

"After two long years of construction, I sure hope there's something good to see inside," announced Kaylin.

Avery, ignoring Kaylin's comment, lifted her hand to shade her eyes as she stared up at the massive structure. "It's amazing how all the lines and angles come together so artistically. The builders sure knew what they were doing."

The stoplight that slowed their progress turned green.

"Quit wasting your time looking on the outside, Avery; it's the inside we came to see. Since it is opening day, I'm sure there will be a crowd. So, let's hurry."

Avery, not wanting to be rushed, grabbed Kaylin's arm. "Hey, let's look at this plaque on the corner of the building. See it there on the brick, near the sidewalk? What a funny place to put a plaque."

"What does it say?"

"'The cornerstone upon which a great work of art will be placed,'" read Avery. "Then there is a date," Avery continued. "I bet it is the date the builders started the construction of the museum."

"Who cares about a cornerstone?" wondered Kaylin.

"Hey, if you don't have a good foundation with the right cornerstone in place, the building will be all crooked and unstable.

This museum looks so good on the outside because they started right with this cornerstone."

"How come you know so much about cornerstones?" Kaylin wondered as she pulled Avery toward the front door of the museum.

"I learned all about it in Sunday school."

"What? Why would they be talking about the museum there?"

"They weren't talking about the museum but about cornerstones. Jesus Christ is called the Chief Cornerstone. If you start your Christian faith with Jesus and build your foundation on the teachings of the Bible, then you will have a great faith that will grow into something beautiful."

Kaylin giggled as they walked through the front door.

"I never thought I would learn something about Jesus at the museum. Come on, let's see if you can teach me something about God in the modern art section!"

Built on the foundation of the apostles and prophets, with Christ Jesus himself as the chief cornerstone.

Ephesians 2:20

What About You?

Have you built your faith on Jesus and the teachings of the Bible, or have you laid a weaker foundation?

Like . . .

- Believing your friend's views are more important than what God teaches?

- Believing your sports hero's thoughts on life mean more than what Jesus taught?

- Believing religious rules rather than making a relationship with Jesus a priority?

Take Time to Pray!

Ask God to help you learn what the Bible has to say rather than what others have to say concerning Jesus and your faith.

Day 29

MY GOD IS MY COUNSELOR

Read: Psalm 16:7

"Get out of my room, and don't ever touch my computer!" Aaron screamed as he slammed his bedroom door behind his little brother, Justin.

"I hate it when he ignores my rules," Aaron continued to rant as he whipped his sweatshirt across the room. Picking up his football, he heaved it at his door, wishing it was Justin's head. Hoping Justin could still hear him, Aaron bellowed his final threat. "I'm going to seriously hurt you if you ever step foot in my room again!"

Justin's silence fueled Aaron's anger as he retrieved his football and then searched for somewhere else to heave it. Across the room, his eyes fell on a large poster that hung above his desk. The black poster highlighted a wooden cross set at an odd angle. Piercing the cross was a dagger dripping with blood. Yet it wasn't this dramatic picture that caught Aaron's attention; it was the words written beneath the cross: *But you, Lord, are a compassionate and gracious God, slow to anger, abounding in love and faithfulness. Psalm 86:15.*

Aaron dropped to his bed, recognizing what God was trying to tell him. "I know, God. You have every reason to be angry with the way we treat You; and still, you are full of compassion and love. Thank You for the reminder that You expect the same from me."

> *I will praise the LORD, who counsels me,*
> *even at night my heart instructs me.*
>
> Psalm 16:7

What About You?

God counsels us through the Bible. There are verses for each of our issues, concerns, and challenges.

Like...

- "[Speak] the truth in love . . . " (Eph. 4:15).

- "Do not let any unwholesome talk come out of your mouths . . . " (Eph. 4:29).

- "Be kind . . . to one another, forgiving each other . . . " (Eph. 4:32).

Take Time to Pray!

Choose one of the above Bible verses and talk to God about what needs to change in your life.

Day 30

MY GOD IS MY CREATOR

Read: Revelations 4:11

The McPherson's Thanksgiving began in the usual Thanksgiving way. Avery slept in, cuddled under the covers, with the smell of turkey drifting in from the kitchen. Midmorning, Avery and her two older sisters set the dining room table. Avery's job was to design the centerpiece out of colorful leaves and pinecones.

Once the family settled around the table, Avery's mom set the turkey in front of her husband, while Avery's mouth began to water.

"Let's keep the prayer short today. I can't wait to dig into that turkey," Avery suggested.

"Let's see if we can do better than that, Avery. The turkey can wait. This is our chance to thank our Creator for all He has created," her dad explained.

Avery's mom, now seated at the other end of the table, offered, "Why don't we each take a turn thanking God for one of His creations?"

"Sounds great," Avery's dad agreed.

Joining hands, they bowed their heads and her mom began. "Thanks, God, for the gift of life and specifically for the lives of my three girls."

Riley, with her straight brown hair tucked behind her ears, went next. "Thanks for Cindy, my new best friend."

Sarah, whose face couldn't be seen behind her curls, quickly followed with, "Thanks for Rob, my awesome boyfriend."

Avery's dad cleared his throat, letting Sarah know he was cutting in. "God, You are our great Creator. Thank You for creating trees, so we could have wood to build this wonderful home."

Avery, not missing a beat, concluded the prayer time with, "Oh, and thanks, God, for turkey . . . amen!"

> *"You are worthy, our Lord and God, to receive glory and honor and power, for you created all things . . . "*
> *Revelation 4:11a*

What About You?

What parts of God's creation make you thankful? Like . . .

- Puppy dogs to play with?
- Trees to climb?
- Streams for fishing?

Take Time to Pray!

Thank God for all your favorite parts of His creation and for being such a creative Creator.

Day 31
MY GOD IS DAZZLING

Read: Mark 9:1-4

Aaron skidded around the corner and bounced off the laundry room door. Grabbing his bruised elbow and injured knee, he frantically hobbled forward.

"Wait, Mom, you gotta include my basketball jersey in the wash!"

Aaron's mom turned up her nose at the offending shirt wadded up in the corner of the laundry room.

"Coach Ryder says it must be dazzling white for our championship game tonight. Can you do it, Mom?"

His mom laughed as she bent over and picked up the grimy mess.

"I'll have to use half the bottle of bleach on this sorry excuse for a jersey if you want it to be dazzling by tonight." As Aaron's mom added the bleach to the full load of dirty white clothes, she moved her son back from the washing machine. "If you get any bleach on what you're wearing, you'll have white spots where you didn't want any. It'll take the color right out of your clothes."

Aaron's eyes got bigger as the powerful liquid poured from the white jug. "Hey, Mom, does this guarantee it'll be dazzling by tonight?"

"Aaron, this bleach will help make your jersey white, but only Jesus can produce dazzling white. When Peter, James, and John were with Jesus on the Mount of Transfiguration, they were seeing the Heavenly Jesus shining through His earthly body. Jesus was so dazzling that it even affected what He was wearing."

"Wow! I bet He could psych out the other team in clothes like that!" Aaron laughed as his mom shut the lid to the washing machine and shooed him from the laundry room.

[Jesus'] clothes became dazzling white, whiter than anyone in the world could bleach them.
Mark 9:3

What About You?

Having read Mark 9:1-4, ask yourself, *What would you have said to Jesus if you were Peter, and you were standing with Jesus on the Mount of Transfiguration when everything about Him became dazzling white?*
Like...

- Wow, You really are God?
- This is amazing; nobody else could do this?
- Cool, if You can do this, You can do anything?

Take Time to Pray!

Tell Jesus your Mount of Transfiguration thought right now.

Day 32

MY GOD IS MY DEFENDER

Read: Isaiah 51:22

Beep! Beep! Beep!

Trevor swatted his alarm clock, ending the irritating sound that signaled it was time to get up. Aaron had invited Trevor to help with the annual church Christmas food drive. They planned on collecting cans of food door-to-door for the entire Saturday morning. As difficult as it was, Trevor managed to get himself out of bed; pull on jeans, a shirt, and a jacket; run a comb through his hair; and get out to the end of his driveway just before Aaron and Mr. March pulled up in front of his house.

"Are you ready to go begging?" Aaron teased as Trevor dropped into the back seat and slammed the car door.

"Just as long as the people at the doors know it's not for me but for the needy families, I think I'll be fine with begging," Trevor answered honestly.

When they arrived at the church, Steve was already organizing the youth. Kaylin and Avery had already been assigned their streets. Aaron quickly asked Steve if he and Trevor could do the same streets as Kaylin and Avery, just on the opposite side.

Steve grinned. "Want to create a little competition, do you?"

Aaron smirked as he gave Trevor a high five. "Male domination for a good cause!"

Steve dropped the four friends off at their first street, and the collecting began. At the end of the road, the pairs stopped to calculate who had collected the most cans. The girls had two dozen, and the guys had ten.

"Watch us in action at this next house," Trevor bragged. "The guy will be so moved, he'll empty his pantry for us."

"Okay." Kaylin laughed. "We'll wait on the sidewalk to see if we can learn anything–anything at all."

The girls stood under the leafless branches of the maple tree while the guys rang the doorbell. Instantly, the door flung open.

"Don't like kids and don't like beggars," the craggy, old man growled.

"We're from the neighborhood church; and we're collecting cans of food for the needy. Would you like to help?" Trevor ventured.

"You four look as needy as they come." The crotchety man squinted toward the girls and then back to the boys again. "I know kids today. You only think of yourselves. A church group—what a lousy cover-up. Get off my property before I call the police."

The door slammed in the guys' faces before they could respond. Stunned, they joined the girls on the sidewalk.

"Boy, I'd like to tell that guy a thing or two," Trevor grumbled. "I got out of bed early to get yelled at. I could have stayed home for that."

"Who's going to put that old man in his place?" Avery demanded.

"Not us," admitted Aaron. "My guess is God is going to have to defend us because nobody else can."

"Maybe it's best God defends us. I think that guy would pick a fight with anybody else," Kaylin shared as she and Avery grabbed their box and moved to the other side of the street.

"Oh great, another thing to leave in God's hands. I sure hope He has big hands," Trevor said with a shrug.

"The biggest!" Aaron promised as the guys moved on to the next house.

Your Sovereign LORD says, your God, who defends his people.

Isaiah 51:22

What About You?

Do you find it easy or difficult to allow God to defend you in a tough situation?

Like . . .

- When you hear a rumor about yourself, but you don't know |who started it?
- When an adult thinks you did something wrong and won't let you explain?
- When you do a kind act, but someone else gets credit for it?

Take Time to Pray!

Ask God to help you remember that He will defend you. Thank Him for always being willing to defend you when you are not in the wrong, even if that defense doesn't happen right away.

Day 33

MY GOD IS DELIGHTED

Read: Psalm 149:4

Exhausted, Kaylin shuffled through her front door, slid over the back of the black leather couch, and landed in a heap on the cushions. Kaylin's mother, sitting in the wing-backed chair facing the couch and front door, never lifted her eyes from her book.

Kaylin sighed deeply. "It was a long but good day, Mom."

Silence followed.

"Mom," Kaylin said a little louder, "I collected cans of food for the needy today."

Her mom set down her book and let her eyes focus on Kaylin. "Collected cans? Were you with that church group again?"

Kaylin laughed as she rolled over and stared at the cathedral ceiling.

"Yeah, Avery and I had a competition with Aaron and Trevor, and we creamed them! We collected 121; they collected sixty-two." Kaylin looked over at her mother, hoping for a response; but her mom had returned to her book.

Kaylin shrugged, then lifted herself from the couch and slowly climbed the stairs lining their side wall. She prayed silently as she walked down the hall that led to her bedroom, *I sure am glad, God, that You delight in my accomplishments.*

For the Lord takes delight in his people . . .

Psalm 149:4

What About You?

What deeds have you done today that have delighted God? Like...

- Showing kindness to a friend?
- Being selfless with a family member?
- Doing your best on a task or job?

Take Time to Pray!

Ask God to help you do things for the rest of today and again tomorrow—things that will bring Him delight.

+ **Day 34** +

MY GOD IS
MY DELIVERER

Read: Psalm 40:17

Avery stumbled into Riley's room loaded down with unwrapped gifts. Finding some room on the carpet closest to the closet, Avery sat down and began to sort through which gift to wrap first. Sarah and Riley were busy wrapping their own gifts as the girls' favorite Christmas music beat out a new rhythm to an old favorite.

"Hey, can you pass a cookie and the green wrapping paper, Riley?" Avery asked from across the room.

"You can get up and get it yourself. I'm not your servant!" Riley retorted as she tucked her hair behind her ears.

"Wow, someone's in a good mood," Avery snarled in her sister's direction.

Sarah, not wanting to be left out, threw her comment into the mix. "Avery, we were having lots of fun before you got here. Why don't you go to your own room to wrap your gifts?"

"Because this is a tradition! We always wrap our gifts together."

"Yeah, well, you're so immature, you ruin our fun just by walking into the room," Sarah snapped.

"I just wanted the paper and a cookie."

"We didn't hear a please," Riley reminded her.

Avery got up and grabbed the paper, tape, and the plate of cookies. Then she stomped back to her place by the closet.

Just then, their mom passed by the room. "I love to see my three girls wrapping their gifts together. This is Christmas to me—family time, laughter, sharing, and cookies. Have fun, girls!" Their mom smiled and then continued down the hall.

None of the girls dared to look up as they stopped the gift wrapping and listened to the song playing from Sarah's phone.

May this Christmas be a time of peace, a time of joy and love / As you celebrate the gift of life sent down from God above.

"Sorry, Avery, we're glad you're here with us," Sarah confessed.

"Yeah," added Riley, "it would mess up our family tradition if you went to your own room; but you could pass back the plate of cookies."

Avery smiled as she shoved the plate toward Riley.

Thank You, God, Avery prayed silently, *for delivering me from conflict through my mom's words. You fixed what I couldn't.*

> *You are my help and my deliverer; you are my God...*
> Psalm 40:17

What About You?

God is great at delivering us from difficult situations. Do you recognize God's deliverance when someone unexpectedly shows up and makes things right?

Like...

- When a friend speaks up and defends you in a fight?
- When something unexpected happens that keeps you from saying something you shouldn't?
- When a teacher asks you to help with a task that eventually helps you understand your schoolwork better?

Take Time to Pray!

Stop and think: has God delivered you from a difficult situation this week? Thank Him for being your Deliverer!

Day 35

MY GOD IS DISPLEASED

Read: I Thessalonians 2:15-16

Mr. and Mrs. March said goodbye to Aaron, Justin, and Trevor, reminding them to be good and that they would be back by 10:00 p.m. The boys, engrossed in the final minutes of their TV show, waved an absent goodbye in response. A few minutes later, their program was over; and a commercial for the latest game captured their attention.

"Wow, Crypt and Crime-Stoppers has got to be mine this Christmas," announced Trevor.

"It *is* going to be mine," Aaron said with a sly smile.

"What?" questioned Trevor. "You know something. I can tell by the look on your face."

Aaron leaned in toward Trevor, willing to share his secret.

"Justin and I did some snooping last week, and we found our stash of Christmas gifts. Sitting on the top of the bag was Crypt and Crime-Stoppers!"

"Ah, man, I've got to see this. You're always so lucky. Come on, let me see what else you're getting."

The three boys raced back to Aaron's parents' bedroom with Aaron in the lead. Justin dove onto the bed as Aaron threw open the closet door and dragged the large green bag into the center of the room. All three boys were laughing it up as they grabbed for the game.

"What are you doing?" screamed a chilling voice.

The question made the three boys jump as they turned toward the bedroom door. Aaron's mom was standing in the doorway, horrified at the scene before her.

"Aaron and Justin, you can go to your rooms. Trevor, Mr. March will drive you home. You can explain to him why you're not spending the night."

"Mom," gasped Aaron. "I . . . we didn't think you would be back so soon."

"Obviously, Aaron, but I forgot my purse. I guess God knew I needed to be home to catch you guys in the act."

The boys left the bedroom as Mrs. March dragged the bag of gifts back into the closet.

A few moments later, Aaron's mom leaned into his room. With a tear-streaked face and a shaky voice, she shared with her oldest son, "You have broken my heart and God's heart with this dishonesty. However, what kind of example have you been for Trevor, who is not a Christian yet? Your actions tonight make it difficult to share your faith with Trevor, and that displeases God."

"Mom, I'm sorry!"

"Sorry you got caught or sorry you were dishonest?"

Aaron remained silent as his mom shut the bedroom door.

> *They [displeased] God . . . in their effort to keep us from speaking to the Gentiles so that they may be saved . . .*
>
> *I Thessalonians 2:15-16a*

What About You?

Are there times when you behave in such a way that it makes it difficult to share your faith with someone who doesn't know God? Like . . .

- When you lie to a teacher?
- When you cheat on a test?
- When you lose your temper?

Take Time to Pray!

Ask God to help you make these wrongs right by saying you are sorry to whomever you have offended.

Day 36
MY GOD IS DIVINE

Read: Romans 1:20

Surrounded by crumpled wrapping paper, scattered bows, and lovely gifts, Avery sighed as she stared contentedly at the star that leaned awkwardly at the top of the Christmas tree.

"Boy, that star is sitting crooked," Avery's dad observed as he began to clean up the Christmas morning mess. "We must have hit the tree when we were retrieving your mom's gift. It is sad that most people miss the star and its message, whether it's tilting awkwardly on top of the tree or shining brightly two thousand years ago," her dad reflected.

"Why is it, Dad, that people miss the message that Jesus was God's Son, Who came to earth to be our Savior?" Avery questioned while organizing her gifts to take to her room.

Avery's dad continued to collect the garbage as he explained, "It's easier for most people to think of Jesus as a baby than as the Divine Son of God, our Savior. Now, Christmas is all about Santa and his gifts, rather than Jesus and His gift of new life through His Son, Who was born in a manger."

"Don't get me wrong," Avery corrected, "I love the gifts; and I still like to leave milk and cookies out for Santa, even though I know who eats them." She giggled. "But Christmas would seem empty without the special story that Jesus, God's Divine Son, chose to come to earth, to live among us and then to die for us. That's what makes Christmas special."

Avery's dad straightened and stared at his daughter whose arms were loaded down with gifts.

"But you don't mind the gifts, do you?" He chuckled.
"Hey, if you're willing to give them, then I'm happy to get them!"

For since the creation of the world God's invisible qualities—his eternal power and divine nature—have been clearly seen...

Romans 1:20a

What About You?

During the Christmas season, find ways to make sure you spend some time celebrating the Christ part of Christmas.

Like...

- Sharing the true Christmas story with a friend.
- Reading the Christmas story beside the tree.
- Giving Jesus a gift of service like baking cookies for a senior shut-in or a lonely neighbor.

Take Time to Pray!

Thank Jesus for coming to earth as a little baby. Thank Him for being willing to live among sinful people. Thank Jesus Christ for being the most important part of Christmas.

Day 37

MY GOD IS ENCOURAGING

Read: II Thessalonians 2:16-17

Kaylin giggled as she stood nervously in her apartment hallway, waiting to be let into the Richards' New Year's Eve party. The apartment door flew open; and immediately, McCall began to bounce on her toes, squealing that it was Kaylin. Christi, dressed in a long, red evening gown, came up behind her curly-haired daughter and motioned for Kaylin to come in. Christi leaned close to Kaylin, so she could be heard over the music.

"Are your parents going to make it?" Christi wondered.

"They're going to try, but I wouldn't count on them showing up." Kaylin shrugged as she continued. "But thanks for inviting me."

McCall quickly grabbed her babysitter's hand.

"Come on, the drinks are in the kitchen; and there is great food covering the dining room table."

"Are there any other kids here?" Kaylin mused aloud while she closed the kitchen door, hoping to block out some of the music.

"My cousin is here. He's your age, and he's playing computer games in my mom's office on the second-floor landing. He's nice. Want to grab some food and join him?"

Kaylin laughed aloud.

"Did I say something funny?" McCall wondered as she poured herself a glass of juice.

"No, I'm laughing at God's sense of humor. I was a little nervous about coming to this party alone; and now I have you, lots of great food, and a nice guy I can play computer games with. I asked God for a little encouragement, and He came through big time for me!"

"Yeah, well, just don't forget me in all your New Year's celebrating, okay, Kaylin?"

"You've got a deal!" Kaylin patted McCall's shoulder as they went to check out the food.

> *May our Lord Jesus Christ himself and God our Father, who ... gave us eternal encouragement and good hope, encourage your hearts ...*
> *II Thessalonians 2:16-17*

What About You?

God is a God of encouragement, Who encourages us every day. Do you notice His encouragement?

Like ...

- When you read a Bible verse, and you feel better?

- When you hear a worship song, and it brings a smile to your face?

- When your parents or friends tell you what a great job you are doing?

Take Time to Pray!

Think of the encouragement God has given to you today (including this devotional). Thank God for the ways He encourages you.

Day 38

MY GOD IS ENTHRONED

Read: Psalm 29:10

Trevor had been listening all fall to Aaron, Avery, and Kaylin's pleas to try out the church youth group, The Bridge. Finally, he gave in; but Trevor wondered what he was getting himself into as he climbed the stairs to the front door of the church.

"Trevor, hurry up, it's freezing out here," Aaron called to his friend, who was lagging behind.

"I don't mind collecting cans for the church food drive. But going to a service about God on a Friday night? That's weird."

"It's not a service, and it's not weird," Aaron said as he pushed Trevor through the door.

Steve greeted Trevor enthusiastically. "Hey, guys, just in time. Head upstairs to the youth room; we have some de-throning to do!"

When Trevor walked into the youth room, he doubled over in laughter at the sight before him. In the center of the room, there was a black tarp covered in a huge pile of pillows. In the center of the pillows was a table with a toilet sitting on top.

Trevor didn't have to wonder what was up for long. Steve rallied the teens together and lined up the youth leaders across one end of the room. As the teens were getting seated, Avery and Kaylin made sure they plopped themselves down just behind Aaron and Trevor.

Avery gave Trevor a playful shove. "Finally decided to check out our youth group, did ya?"

Trevor shrugged, then turned to listen to Steve. "Okay, the loudest cheer decides which youth leader sits on the throne." Steve began saying the different leaders' names; but when he said his own, the crowd went wild.

"Your king is chosen. The question is how long will I stay enthroned? Each of you will grab a pillow to throw at me—if you find a free pillow near you, throw it! I will climb to the throne blindfolded while you pummel me with pillows. The clock will be running to see if I make it to the throne and how long I will stay on the throne. To make it even more challenging, my hands must remain above my head; or I'm disqualified."

The pillows were grabbed amidst hoots and hollers. Steve was blindfolded, and the stopwatch began. Pillows went flying. Steve had three minutes to get to the throne and then to stay on the throne before his turn was over. Halfway up, he fell off the table and landed in a heap on the pillows that hadn't been picked up. A roar of laughter went up from the crowd.

Each youth leader attempted the same climb, and each was dethroned before the three-minute timer went off. Forty-five minutes later, the last leader had been dethroned. Steve settled the group to explain to them that there is one King Who can never be dethroned, and that is Jesus Christ.

At the end of the night, Steve made sure he invited Trevor again to The Bridge. Trevor raised one eyebrow and smirked in response. "I have never seen church done this way. Yeah, I'll come back again."

> *The LORD sits enthroned over the flood;*
> *the LORD is enthroned as King forever.*
>
> *Psalm 29:10*

What About You?

Can you think of times when you try to dethrone God in your own life?

Like...

- When you ignore His rules?
- When you misuse His name?
- When you love other things more than God—like friends, sports, or TV?

Take Time to Pray!

God is God and will always remain enthroned on His Heavenly throne. We need to recognize this and treat him like the King He is! Thank Him for being King and ask Him to help you keep Him enthroned in your own life.

Day 39

MY GOD IS EQUIPPING

Read: Hebrews 13:20-21

Avery was cutting across the church foyer in search of her sister, Riley, when the Kid's Community director stepped in front of her. Mrs. Rollins' sweet smile greeted Avery.

"Young lady, your mom was telling me that one of your New Year's resolutions is to serve more in the church. I was wondering if you wanted to start next Sunday by leading a small group of four-year-olds for a fifteen-minute story time?"

Avery, stunned by the request, stared open-mouthed at Mrs. Rollins.

"Me . . . t-t-teach a Bible story?" Avery stammered.

"I think you would be wonderful," Mrs. Rollins assured Avery. "Besides, I believe God has equipped you with the gift of teaching. I've been watching you over the last couple of years as you've taken many opportunities to teach the children of our church how to climb the church stairs, tie their shoes, or even spit watermelon seeds at the church picnic. Now, you have a chance to use your gift to teach the Bible."

"You think God has been preparing me, actually equipping me, to teach the Bible?" Avery mused, half distracted by Aaron, who had stopped behind Mrs. Rollins to eavesdrop on the conversation.

Mrs. Rollins, unaware of Aaron, quickly responded, "Of course, God equips us for every job He wants us to do."

Aaron silently howled at Avery for being chosen as a small group storyteller until Avery piped up, "Hey, Mrs. Rollins, didn't I hear you say last week that you needed someone to dress up like Super Bible Man for next Sunday's Kid's Community Bible Quiz?"

"Why, yes, I did," Mrs. Rollins replied.

Aaron stopped his silent laughter as Avery offered, "How about Aaron? I know he'd look great in that red Super Bible Man costume!"

Aaron turned to run, but Avery was too quick. Reaching behind Mrs. Rollins, Avery grabbed Aaron's sleeve, stopping him in his tracks.

"Hey, look, Mrs. Rollins, here he is now. Hey, Aaron, Mrs. Rollins has something to ask you."

Aaron shot Avery a look, then turned and smiled at Mrs. Rollins, knowing that next week he was going to be Super Bible Man.

Now may the God of peace . . .
equip you with everything good for doing his will . . .
Hebrews 13:20-21

What About You?

For what kind of job is God equipping you?
Like . . .

- Helping with the church yard work?

- Working in your Kid's Community program, doing singing, crafts, or teaching?

- Setting up chairs, collecting the offering, or decorating for special services?

Take Time to Pray!

Ask God to help you see how He is equipping you to serve at your church. Then get involved in serving God!

Day 40
MY GOD IS ETERNAL

Read: Romans 1:20

The next Sunday blew bitterly cold as Avery ran into the church, wrapped in her winter coat. Aaron met her in his red Super Bible Man costume.

"Look at me! I look like a piece of licorice," Aaron complained as Avery peeled off her coat, hat, and scarf.

"That's what you get for making fun of me."

"Come on, let's head to Kid's Community before any more people arrive." Aaron glanced around, then grabbed Avery's arm.

Mrs. Rollins greeted Avery and Aaron with her usual sweet smile. "Aaron, you look great! Avery, are you ready for your first lesson?"

Avery groaned as she plopped into a kiddy chair beside the craft table. Shaking her head, she flipped open her Bible and then looked up at Mrs. Rollins.

"Tough first lesson, Mrs. Rollins. I have to help four-year-old kids understand that God is eternal—that He was never born and will never die. I have trouble understanding that concept, so how will I ever help a four-year-old child understand it?"

Mrs. Rollins pulled up another chair and joined Avery as Aaron sat down on the table. He seemed curious to hear Mrs. Rollins answer, too.

"Avery, your job is to share the truth. There are some aspects of God we won't really understand until we get to Heaven. The concept of God being eternal requires some faith for me, for you, and for the four-year-old children you will be teaching."

"Well," said Aaron, as he leaped up, "after hearing what you have to teach, Avery, I'm glad to say I only have to be Super Bible Man!" With his last words, Aaron soared from the classroom in search of kids to make laugh.

> *For since the creation of the world God's invisible qualities—his eternal power and divine nature—have been clearly seen...*
> Romans 1:20

What About You?

It is so important to accept the truth that God is eternal! When we trust that God is eternal, it helps us realize other truths about Him. Like...

- He wouldn't be God if someone created Him.

- He wouldn't be God if, by accident, He just happened to be made.

- He wouldn't be God if, one day, He got too old and died.

Take Time to Pray!

Thank God that although you can't fully understand that He has no beginning and no end, you still accept the truth that He is eternal; and you are glad He is God.

Day 41

MY GOD IS EVERLASTING

Read: Isaiah 40:28

Seven four-year-old children settled on the floor, ready to hear their Bible lesson. A little red-headed boy with freckles reached over and pulled the pigtail of a girl sitting at the front of the group.

"Billy, leave Ty'esha alone," Avery corrected, as she pulled out a Tootsie Pop and handed it to the upset girl. Pulling off the wrapper, the girl stuck the candy in her mouth and replaced the scowl with a smile. All the kids stared at her until Billy broke the silence.

"Hey, teacher, don't we get a Tootsie Pop, too?"

Avery tilted her head and shrugged. "Well, let me ask you a few questions. Will that Tootsie Pop last forever?"

"No!" the kids all agreed.

"Why not?"

"Because it's supposed to be eaten," the girl in the pigtails mumbled around the sweet treat.

Avery reached down into her bag and pulled out a daisy. "Will this flower last forever?"

"No!" the children answered.

"Why not?"

Billy was ready for this question. "Because you picked it and flowers always die."

Avery smiled as she set the flower in a waiting vase. Turning back to the small group, Avery asked, "Will Billy always be pulling pigtails?"

The group was not so quick to answer. Billy giggled as he tried to reach for the closest pigtail. The blonde, who was Billy's next victim, piped up, "Teacher, my mom says that someday, Billy will stop pulling pigtails because he'll grow up and want to date girls instead of bug girls."

"No way!" Billy gagged.

Avery laughed, ready to make her point. "The truth is the Tootsie Pop will get eaten; the flower will die; and Billy will eventually stop bugging girls. But there is one thing that will never change—there is one thing that will always be the same—and that is God. He is called everlasting because He will last forever; He will always be God. Isn't it great to know we have a God like that?"

"Yes," the children agreed; then a cheer went up as each received their own Tootsie Pop.

> *Do you not know? Have you not heard?*
> *The LORD is the everlasting God . . .*
> Isaiah 40:28a

What About You?

How do you feel about the fact that people and/or things will eventually die, be ruined, or break?

Like . . .

- Sadness over a grandparent who is ill?
- Frustration over a broken bike or damaged piece of sporting equipment?
- Anger over your favorite outfit that has a permanent stain?

Take Time to Pray!

You never need to experience those emotions of sadness, frustration, or anger concerning God. Thank Him for remaining perfect forever!

Day 42
MY GOD IS EXALTED

Read: Psalm 108:5

First thing Saturday morning, Aaron jumped out of bed and pulled up the blinds, hoping to find what the weatherman had promised. He was not disappointed; his backyard was covered in snow. Grabbing the phone, Aaron called Trevor, knowing he would wake him.

"Hello?" Trevor answered groggily.

"Trev, get up; the snow has arrived."

"Snow?"

"Hey, it's time to put into action Plan Sabotage. Get your sorry self out of bed and meet me in the bushes across from Avery's house."

"Okay, okay, I'll be there in twenty minutes." True to his word, Trevor came sneaking around the corner and dove into the bushes beside Aaron.

"What are the girls doing out in the front yard? I thought we were going to pound Avery's bedroom window with snowballs. Now what are we going to do?" wondered Trevor.

"Are you kidding? This is better! We can attack Avery and Kaylin with snowballs while they finish building that silly snowman."

While Aaron and Trevor stockpiled snowballs, Avery and Kaylin were putting the finishing touches on their snowman.

"Hey, Avery, look at this broken branch; the prongs make it look like a crown. Let's make our snowman a snow king," suggested Kaylin.

Avery finished smoothing the top ball on the snowman; then she stood back and surveyed their Saturday morning project.

"He looks good enough to be a king. Go ahead and crown him," Avery cooed.

Just as Kaylin put the branch in place, Trevor and Aaron charged from their hiding place, letting their snowballs fly.

Kaylin and Avery, totally taken off guard, jumped behind their snow king.

"Bring down the king!" the boys chanted as they threw the snowballs. When their arsenal was empty, the guys began high-fiving their success. The snow-covered girls peeked out from behind their snowman.

"Hey, you knocked off his head and his crown," Avery accused.

Trevor, howling at their success, went over to lean against the snowman, knocking off the middle ball.

"Hey, Avery," Aaron said, "you should know by now that there is only one King, exalted above all else. Your snow king is now a snow mound."

Avery turned to Kaylin and slowly smiled. "Let's get 'em!"

With that, the snowballs really began to fly!

Be exalted, O God, above the heavens . . .

Psalm 108:5a

What About You?

Think of different ways you can exalt God as King in your life. *Like . . .*

- Telling Him how wonderful He is.
- Obeying His commands given in the Bible.
- Telling others about Him and His salvation through Jesus.

Take Time to Pray!

Get creative in the way you pray. Think of how many ways God is the best—He is exalted above everyone else. Share with Him your list.

Day 43

MY GOD IS FAITHFUL

Read: I Corinthians 10:13

Kaylin sat at her kitchen table, staring through her high-rise apartment windows at the city. Avery had challenged her to memorize some of God's promises. The colored cards on which Avery had recorded the verses sat before Kaylin on the table. She was determined to memorize at least one of the verses before she watched the movie she had selected for the evening.

The pink card was her first verse. "'Never will I leave you; never will I forsake you.'"[1] The yellow card was Kaylin's favorite verse, which came from the book of Philippians: "And my God will meet all your needs according to the riches of his glory in Christ Jesus."[2] However, the verse Kaylin knew she needed the most was the blue card that sat right in the center: "No temptation has overtaken you except what is common to mankind. And God is faithful; he will not let you be tempted beyond what you can bear. But when you are tempted, he will also provide a way out so that you can endure it."[3]

Kaylin's fingers tapped the table as she thought over this last verse. She knew the movie she was planning to watch was not a good movie. Her parents wouldn't care, but she knew God would not be pleased.

"Is this Your way of being faithful to me, God?" Kaylin wondered aloud. "Is this Your way of getting me out of this temptation by

---
1 Hebrews 13:5
2 Philippians 4:19
3 I Corinthians 10:13

having me work on memorizing these verses before I start the movie?" Kaylin grabbed the blue card and pushed back from the table. "You win. No movie tonight. I will go upstairs, memorize my verse, and then finish reading my book."

With a smile, Kaylin moved through the living room and climbed the stairs, knowing that God had been faithful to help her make the right decision.

> *No temptation has overtaken you except what is common to mankind. And God is faithful...*
> *I Corinthians 10:13a*

What About You?

God promises to be faithful to you. This means He will be faithful to be with you, to meet all your needs, and even to help you avoid temptation. Do you see God's faithfulness in your life?

Like...

- When He sends a Christian friend or family member to remind you about what He wants you to do?

- When you sit down to eat dinner and see all the food in front of you that God provided?

- When, with God's help, you manage to say no to doing something wrong?

Take Time to Pray!

Thank God for His faithfulness in keeping His promises to you.

Day 44

MY GOD IS MY FATHER

Read: II Corinthians 6:18

The pots and pans clattered in the kitchen. In the living room, Trevor, who was shoved into the corner of the couch watching TV, struggled to ignore his mom's racket. The noise and angry words grew in intensity, and Trevor knew he needed to see what was upsetting his mom. Getting up from the couch, he stuck his head into the kitchen and watched while his mom ripped apart the head of lettuce.

"Trouble, Mom?"

Trevor's mom whipped around, tears streaming down her face.

"Your dad called."

"He's still alive, is he?" Trevor asked sarcastically as he leaned against the doorframe.

"It would be better if he were dead—that way I wouldn't have to listen to him every six months—or whenever he decides to pick up a phone and call," Trevor's mom continued to rant as she returned to her salad.

Trevor shrugged as he pulled his phone out of his back pocket and went down the hall to his bedroom. Without wasting time, he called Aaron.

"What's up?" Aaron answered.

"A better question is, 'Who's not around?' And the answer would be 'my dad.'"

"Is your mom upset?"

"That's putting it mildly," Trevor conceded, as he dropped onto his bed.

"Man, I wish you could see that God wants to be your Father; and He's a perfect Father, Who will never let you down."

"Aaron, it's hard for me to think of God as a perfect Father when I have such a lousy earthly father." A noise from the kitchen distracted Trevor from the conversation. "Sorry, Aaron, my mom is yelling for my help. I'd better go. Thanks for listening."

As Trevor hung up, he wondered what it would be like to have a perfect father.

*"I will be a Father to you,
and you will be my sons and daughters, says the Lord Almighty."*
II Corinthians 6:18

What About You?

Are there times when you confuse your earthly father's mistakes with your Heavenly Father's ways?

Like . . .

- When your dad seems too busy to listen, and you figure God doesn't want to hear from you either?

- When your dad spends too many late nights at work, and you figure God isn't around either?

- When your dad gets angry at an innocent mistake, and you wonder if God is angry, too?

Take Time to Pray!

Thank God for being the perfect Heavenly Father.

Day 45
MY GOD IS TO BE FEARED

Read: Psalm 76:6-7

Aaron shoved his little brother aside as the two tried to enter the back door together. Justin fell sideways, and the weight of his backpack carried him into the leafless rose bush that decorated the back door entrance.

"Ow! You did that on purpose, Aaron!" Justin whined as they entered the kitchen. He called to his mom, "I'm bleeding, Aaron pushed me into the rose bush."

Their mom entered the kitchen just as Aaron turned around and hissed at his brother, "Will you be quiet, you little baby? It's your fault for having such a heavy backpack."

Justin pushed past Aaron as tears began to run down his cheeks. "Mom, look at what Aaron did."

"Hey, I didn't touch the little creep!"

Their mom raised her hand to stop Aaron before he said anything more he would regret. "Justin, go to the medicine cabinet and put some antibiotic cream on those scratches; use some band-aids if you need them. Aaron, you can stay here for a moment."

Justin left the kitchen sniffling as Aaron groaned under his breath. "Mom, I didn't do anything wrong!"

"Aaron, you lied; you were selfish; you called your brother a name; you were impatient; you pushed your brother; and then you didn't have enough compassion to feel sorry for what you did. I saw you at the back door while I was watching from the laundry room window. I heard what you had to say to your brother once you entered the kitchen. Yet even more importantly, God saw you; and He heard you. You need to respect and fear God enough to do better than what you just did. A holy God just witnessed an unholy act, and that displeases Him."

"Okay, Mom," said Aaron as he slung his backpack over his shoulder. "I'll go say sorry to Justin and see if I can help him with the Band-Aids; and while I'm walking there, I'll say sorry to God."

God ... It is you alone who are to be feared ...
Psalm 76:6-7a

What About You?

Do you fear (respect) God enough to stop yourself before you do something that will displease Him?

Like ...

- Telling a lie?
- Being selfish?
- Lacking self-control?

Take Time to Pray!

Ask God to help you become more aware of your sin. Say sorry for any sins you have done recently that still need to be confessed.

Day 46
MY GOD IS FLAWLESS

Read: Proverbs 30:5

Kaylin's eyes lit up as she spotted Avery across the gym. The crowd of students huddling around the art displays made it challenging for Kaylin to get to Avery. When Kaylin finally squeezed through the crowd, she was able to nudge Avery as the artist began to describe his sculpture to the surrounding group.

"The piece of marble I started with was flawless, giving scope to my creativity. Having no faults riveting the stone enabled my inner urges and vision to be realized in this masterpiece I call *Serendipity*."

The artist flung his long hair out of his eyes while speaking those last words, and Kaylin couldn't help but giggle at what she had just witnessed. While the artist took some questions, Kaylin whispered into Avery's ear, "Did you understand what the artist just said?"

Avery turned away from the sculpture with a smirk on her face.

"I had no idea urges and visions could be poured into a piece of marble, but I would love to challenge the artist on his 'flawless' comment. Only one Person is flawless, and that is the Creator of the piece of marble."

"You don't think things in creation can be flawless?"

"Maybe in the Garden of Eden and Heaven, but not here on earth. It's amazing to think we will see a flawless God when we get to Heaven, though!" Avery smiled.

"Every word of God is flawless..."
Proverbs 30:5

What About You?

Have you ever looked at an object and thought it was perfect and didn't have any flaws, then realized that there was a weakness?

Like...

- A car that eventually has engine trouble?
- A flower that withers and dies?
- A cute puppy that chews shoes?

Take Time to Pray!

Thank God for being flawless. Tell Him how grateful you are that no matter how close you look at Him, you will never find anything short of perfection!

Day 47

MY GOD IS FORGIVING

Read: Colossians 3:13

Inspired by the art displays at school, Avery decided to spend all day Saturday in her garage, creating a few treasures of her own. She planned to spend the morning designing a paper mâché sculpture that came from her internal "urges and vision."

Early in the afternoon, Avery stood back to survey her progress. She had to admit that her sculpture resembled a small alien, but she was confident the end project would be artistically inspiring. Eager to put the second layer of paper and paste on her project, Avery decided to use a blow-dryer to speed up the drying process. Just as Avery felt the sculpture was dry enough, Sarah walked in the side door of the garage.

"Hurry and shut the door, Sarah; you're letting all the cold air in!" Avery yelled as she turned off the blow-dryer.

"What is that supposed to be?" Sarah wondered with a screwed-up face.

"I'm inspired, and this is my work of art," said Avery, beaming.

"I hate to break it to you, but it looks like a mess," Sarah said with a shake of her head as she moved the ladder beside Avery's sculpture.

"And by the way," Sarah continued, while climbing the ladder, "that's my blow-dryer, and I want it back in my bathroom drawer before you do another thing."

Avery wasn't pleased with Sarah's response to her sculpture; but she hoped to borrow the blow-dryer after the second coat of paper mâché, so she decided she had better take it back to the bathroom.

When Avery entered the garage a few minutes later, the sight stopped her in her tracks. Her dad's bowling ball was in the center of her sculpture, having completely crushed her work.

Furious, Avery screamed at her guilty sister, "You ruined my work! Just because you didn't like it doesn't mean you needed to destroy it!"

Sarah quickly climbed down the ladder, stumbling over her words. "Avery, it was an accident. I was looking for the old suitcase; and I accidentally hit the bowling ball, knocking it off the shelf. Will you please forgive me?" Sarah pleaded.

> *Forgive as the Lord forgave you.*
> *Colossians 3:13b*

What About You?

Is there someone in your life you haven't forgiven?
Like . . .

- A friend from school who didn't act like a friend?
- A sister or a brother who ruined something of yours?
- An adult who hasn't been kind?

Take Time to Pray!

Whether they are sorry or not, God still wants us to forgive them the way He has forgiven us. Share with God your hurt and then tell God you forgive them, anyway. You will feel better once you let go of that anger.

Day 48

MY GOD IS MY FRIEND

Read: Matthew 11:19

Valentine's Day is such a waste, all that love and cards and stuff, reflected Trevor to himself as he walked up his dirt driveway. *You don't see anybody loving me, that's for sure.*

He tossed his backpack onto his front porch. A howl erupted from underneath the porch, startling Trevor. Dropping to one knee, Trevor spotted what looked like a Golden Lab puppy curled up under the wooden steps.

"Hey, boy, whatcha doing under there? It's too cold to be out here all on your own." Trevor's soothing voice relaxed the shivering puppy enough so that he could ease him from his hiding spot. Trevor gently tucked the furry bundle inside his coat and then grabbed his backpack and quickly moved inside.

The puppy took a few minutes to sniff around before he began to play tug-a-war with Trevor's backpack. The next two hours were filled with the puppy—bathing and blow-drying him, finding some scraps for him to eat, and laughing at the way he tried to fetch the soccer ball.

After so much activity, the puppy was ready for a nap. Trevor decided to call Aaron and tell him about Mickey. Settled on the couch with Mickey cradled in the crook of his arm, Trevor shared with Aaron all the puppy's antics.

"Yeah, and it's great that the little thing already knows his name."

"Why did you call him Mickey?" Aaron wondered from the other end of the phone.

"Because he's as entertaining as Mickey Mouse."

"Well, you were complaining today that nobody loves you enough to give you a Valentine's gift, but I guess you were wrong. God loves you enough to give you a puppy."

"I don't know about God, but this dog is certainly man's best friend."

"Trevor, you have that backwards. It's not a D-O-G that's man's best friend; it is G-O-D. With this small gift of a puppy, God is trying to tell you that He wants to be your Best Friend."

"Well, Mickey is sure a nice token of God's friendship," Trevor reflected as he looked down at the sleeping bundle breathing softly on his lap.

[Jesus] . . . a friend of . . . sinners.
Matthew 11:19a

What About You?

Have you ever thought about the different ways God proves to you that He is your Best Friend?

Like . . .

- Always being there ready to listen when you pray?
- Always ready to forgive you and love you?
- Always wanting the best for you and willing to help you?

Take Time to Pray!

Tell God what you want in a best friend and then thank Him for being the very Best Friend you could ever have.

Day 49
MY GOD IS GIVING

Read: James 1:17

Trevor's mom dropped onto her couch, exhausted from a long day of waiting tables at the restaurant. She lit a cigarette and blew the smoke at the ceiling, glad for an evening with nothing to do. Suddenly, a ball of yellow fur ran underneath her outstretched legs, sending her screaming from the couch.

"Trevor, there's an animal in the house!" she called in panic.

Trevor appeared in the living room doorway.

"I know, Mom," Trevor soothed. "It's Mickey. Aaron says he is God's Valentine's present to me."

"Trevor, this God thing has gone too far if He has started to giftwrap puppies. Did He appear in the living room and present it to you personally?" his mom asked sarcastically.

"No, God left Mickey huddling under our front porch."

"Well, you can't keep him," Trevor's mom said as she sidestepped the puppy and walked into the kitchen.

"Why not? I bet you didn't get me anything for Valentine's Day. So, let Mickey be my gift from you and God."

His mom blew out another cloud of smoke as she leaned against the kitchen counter and stared down at her son.

"Did you get me anything for Valentine's Day?" she asked.

"No."

"Well, then, we're even. But I'll tell you what—you call the pound; and if nobody is looking for a Golden Lab puppy, then you can keep him. Remember, he's yours to clean up after, care for, and feed."

"Thanks, Mom, I'll call right now," Trevor said as he grabbed his phone and searched for the number. Three minutes later, Trevor tossed the phone on the couch with a whoop, grabbed Mickey, and began tumbling with him on the carpet. "Looks like you're going to be mine!"

Every good and perfect gift is from above...
James 1:17a

What About You?

Are you ready to share with people the truth that everything good in your life comes from God?

Like...

- Your home and family?
- Your car, bike, scooter, etc.?
- Your friendships?

Take Time to Pray!

Begin thanking God for all His good gifts, and don't stop until you've covered them all!

Day 50

MY GOD IS GLORIFIED

Read: Isaiah 66:5

Ms. Phillips waited until the last moment to let out her math class. Trevor rushed to his locker and finished gathering his homework as Aaron sauntered over and leaned against the lockers.

"When do I get to meet Mickey?" Aaron wondered.

"If you can move a little faster, you can come home with me right now. It's been killing me to be away from Mickey all day, so hurry!"

Aaron, respecting Trevor's impatience, went to his locker to gather what he needed for home. Trevor was ready to yell at Aaron to hurry up when he felt a tug on his backpack. Avery and Kaylin were both beaming at Trevor, who scowled back.

Avery spoke first. "Trev, you're supposed to look happy about the end of the school day."

"Oh, I am. I'm just anxious to get home to see Mickey."

Kaylin threw her question into the conversation, "How did you ever get your mom to let you keep the puppy?"

"Aaron says God did that, and I think Aaron is right. The puppy showed up out of nowhere; no one seems to be looking for it; we've put up posters, and nobody has called. So, my mom has said I can keep him. Each one of these things is a miracle. When you put them all together, it looks like something only God could do."

"Hey," Avery interrupted, "it almost sounds like you are starting to believe in God. Actually, I could be wrong, but it sounds like you are giving God the glory for Mickey."

Trevor screwed up his face.

"How can I give God the glory when I don't even know what that means?" Aaron slammed his locker shut.

"It means you're giving God the credit; you're saying God's responsible; and you're happy about it. Now, come on, let's go see this gift from God."

Trevor and Aaron, not wanting to waste another minute inside Glenwood, said goodbye to the girls.

"Let the Lord be glorified..."
Isaiah 66:5b

What About You?

Are you quick to give God the glory for the good things in your life? Like...

- A cold that clears up quickly?
- A chance to make some extra money?
- A new item of clothing?

Take Time to Pray!

Glorify God during your prayer time. Think of the good things that have happened to you and give God the credit and thanks for them.

Day 51

MY GOD IS GOOD

Read: Psalm 34:8

Having finished cleaning up from the evening meal, Aaron's mom called her boys into the kitchen. Aaron and Justin entered the kitchen and immediately wondered about the cloth-covered items lining the kitchen table.

"Don't touch the napkins," his mom warned.

"Go ahead and pull up a seat around the table," she continued with a smile. "Our pastor challenged us with a verse this past Sunday. We were to 'taste and see that the LORD is good.'[4] Well, I thought for family devotions, we should try to understand what that verse means."

"Oh," mumbled Justin, "I thought we were going to do something fun."

"A little taste test competition might be some fun," his mom enthused. Aaron laughed at the excitement in his mom's eyes as she went around to the other side of the table.

"All right, come and line up and get your blindfold; then I will reach under the napkins and give you a sample of the hidden food."

"There's nothing moldy or rotten, is there?" Aaron asked with skepticism as his blindfold was tied in place.

Their dad gave Justin the sample at the same time as their mom gave Aaron his sample. Their reactions made it worth recording on the phone he pulled out of his back pocket. The onion made both boys gag and beg for water. The peppermint candy helped remove the taste of onion. They begged for more potato chips, but their favorite was their mom's homemade chocolate chip cookies.

---

4   Psalm 34:8

"Mmmm, now we're talking yummy," Justin mumbled through a mouthful of cookie.

As Aaron licked his lips, he added, "Mom, your cookies always taste so good."

Removing the boys' blindfolds, their mom explained how this taste test tied in with their memory verse.

"Just like the cookies are good every time you sample them, so God is good all the time. Add all of God's qualities together, and they can be summarized by one phrase: *God is good!* When you consider how God is good, it is like taking a taste test, a test that does not include raw onions."

"Hey, thanks, Mom," Aaron said. "Now I understand that verse better."

"Good." His dad smiled. "Now, would you like to see your faces when you tasted the onions? We were recording you during the taste test, and your faces were priceless."

> *Taste and see that the LORD is good;*
> *blessed is the one who takes refuge in him.*
>
> Psalm 34:8

What About You?

Have you ever thought about how one word sums up God's qualities? That word is *good*.

Like . . .

- Kind plus gentle plus patient equals good.
- Loving plus caring plus generous equals good.
- Forgiving plus compassionate plus holy equals good.

Take Time to Pray!

Look over the Table of Contents for this devotional. The one word to sum up all one hundred character qualities of God is the word *good*. Thank God for being such a good God!

Day 52

MY GOD IS GRACIOUS

Read: Isaiah 30:18

Saturday morning breakfast found the March family still laughing at Aaron and Justin's funny faces their dad had captured the night before. The family was enjoying their usual Saturday morning pancake breakfast, but the boys knew their weekly chores had to be done before they could get on with the rest of the day.

Justin was to clean the bathrooms and then sweep and mop the kitchen floor. Aaron was responsible for the dusting and vacuuming. The boys, having both decided to have another pancake, were still eating as their mom slipped on her spring jacket and their dad grabbed the car keys.

"Boys," Mr. March began, "we'll be gone for an hour or so. All the jobs are to be done before we get back."

"And make sure your breakfast dishes end up in the dishwasher," Mrs. March added.

The boys, with full mouths, nodded and waved as their parents disappeared out the back door.

A few minutes later, the two put their dishes in the dishwasher and were moving to start their jobs when Aaron suggested a video game competition before they began their work. An hour later, they were still playing when their parents walked into the living room.

"All right, boys, we have a surprise for you!" their dad said.

But the smile quickly slipped from their mom's face. "Hold it a minute," she said. "It doesn't look like the vacuuming has been done."

Aaron paused the game as the boys looked at their parents with guilt-ridden faces.

"Oops," Justin mumbled.

"Oops?" repeated their dad. "Aaron, can you do any better than oops?"

"How about 'we're sorry' and 'we'll do them right now'?" Aaron asked as he got to his feet.

"Well, here's a chance for you to understand the word *grace*. Grace means you receive something good when you do not deserve it. Your mom and I are going to choose to be gracious to you both. You didn't do your chores, and you deserve discipline; instead, we are going to take you out on the town in our new car!"

"New car?" Justin questioned.

"We just picked it up. It's in the driveway, waiting."

"No way! What kind of car?" Aaron asked as he jogged toward the back door.

"A black Mustang," Mr. March called after his son. "Get dressed, and we'll take it for a spin!"

Yet the LORD longs to be gracious to you . . .
Isaiah 30:18a

What About You?

Do you recognize when God has been gracious to you? Like . . .

- When you are doing something wrong and instead of getting caught, He lets you learn the lesson on your own?

- When you get in trouble at school for not doing your homework and your parents decide they will take you out for dinner, anyway?

- When God forgives your sins, even when you don't forgive your sister or brother?

Take Time to Pray!

Thank God for being gracious to you. Ask Him to help you to be gracious to others, too.

Day 53
MY GOD IS GREAT

Read: Psalm 145:3

It took Justin and Aaron ten minutes to get cleaned up and dressed for the day.

"This is great!" Aaron exclaimed as he stood beside their new black Mustang, still shiny from the car lot. "Why didn't you tell us about this?" Aaron wondered.

"Your mom and I thought it would be a great surprise."

"Boy, were you right," Aaron said as the two boys climbed into the back seat.

"Great new car smell," Justin added.

"I love the smell of new cars. Dad, do you know how great this is? Hey, let's drive by Trevor's house; he has got to see this."

Both parents were thoroughly enjoying the boy's enthusiasm as they climbed into the front seat and started the car.

"Boys," their mom said as she shifted in her seat so she could see them both, "I've heard you comment on how great this car is; but we would be missing a wonderful opportunity if we didn't point out how great God is. God has given your dad a great year in business. The money he has made makes it possible for us to afford this car. This is God's great gift to us."

Their dad, with his head nodding in agreement, added his thoughts. "Your mother and I want our prayers to be the first thing we do as a family in this car. So, let's each take a moment to thank God for being so great!"

During the prayers, the boys spent a lot of time pointing out to God all the cool qualities of the car; but their parents made sure God's cool qualities were included in their prayer of thanks.

Once they were done praying, their dad grabbed the wheel and shifted into gear. Then he said with a smile, "Let's share the fun of this new car with a few friends; then we can visit the Super Sonic Game Room and play a few games and maybe even get pizza for lunch."

"Sounds like a great way to spend Saturday," Aaron said with a smile as he settled back into the leather seats.

> *Great is the LORD and most worthy of praise;*
> *his greatness no one can fathom.*
>
> Psalm 145:3

What About You?

Great things happen on a daily basis, and they are reflections of our great God.

Like...

- Dew on the grass that helps keep it green.
- A warm sun that feeds the plants.
- Rain that allows the crops to grow.

Take Time to Pray!

A new car is a special "great" gift that doesn't come very often. Yet important and needed gifts like dew, sun, and rain come to us daily from a great God Who knows what we need. Thank God for being great and for giving great gifts.

Day 54

MY GOD IS MY HEALER

Read: Exodus 15:26

The smell of spring was in the air as Avery climbed on top of Rio. The horses in the pasture were frisky. They kicked up their heels, glad that winter would soon be left behind. The outdoor ring was still a bit wet from the spring rains, but Rio seemed able to handle the damp sand. After about twenty minutes of warming up, Avery eyed a low jump set up in the center of the ring and impulsively decided to take it. Rio lined up nicely, and Avery remembered to give him lots of leg as they flew over the jump. Rio landed on the other side and slipped in a puddle Avery had failed to notice. Rio stumbled but recovered his footing without losing Avery off his back.

As soon as Rio came to a stop, Avery dismounted and began running her hand over the injured leg. James, Avery's trainer, came around the corner and propped a foot on the lower rail of the wooden fence that enclosed the ring.

"Hey," James called, "having some trouble, Avery?"

Without letting go of Rio's leg, Avery peeked under her horse's neck at her trainer. "I took the jump without noticing the puddle. Rio slipped on the landing, and now his leg feels hot. I think he's hurt."

"Walk Rio around," James instructed. "I'll watch for a limp."

It only took James a moment to identify Rio's injury. "Take Rio back to the barn, Avery. Your horse is going to need a week or two to recover from his injury," James said with a shake of his head. He held open the large iron gate that was the only exit from the ring.

Twenty minutes later, Avery had finished brushing Rio; and with her head hung low, she led her horse into the stall. Leaning against his neck, Avery softly prayed, "Please, God, heal Rio's leg quickly."

"I am the LORD, who heals you."
Exodus 15:26b

What About You?

Do you recognize it is God Who brings healing to your hurts, injuries, or sicknesses?

Like...

- A broken bone?
- A cut or other injury?
- A broken heart or hurt feelings?

Take Time to Pray!

God is the best doctor. Remember to include Him in the healing process. Ask God to heal someone you know who is hurt but trust His timing and purpose in that healing.

Day 55
MY GOD IS MY HELPER

Read: Hebrews 13:6

Mickey skidded around the corner and tore across the living room to greet Trevor as he came in from school.

"Hey, boy, miss me?" Trevor asked as he grabbed the tennis ball out of Mickey's mouth and threw it into the kitchen.

"Keep that dog out of here!" screamed Trevor's mom as Mickey bumped into a kitchen chair trying to retrieve his ball.

Trevor dropped his backpack on the kitchen table.

"Got anything to eat? I'm starved," he said to his mom as he walked toward the fridge.

"Yeah," his mom shot back, "but you have to find it yourself." She was not about to be distracted from the pan she was cleaning.

Trevor lifted the lid of the pizza box that was shoved onto the top shelf of the fridge. He grabbed a piece of leftover pizza and warmed it in the microwave. His mom finally finished cleaning the pan as Trevor sat down at the table ready to enjoy his afternoon snack.

"Mom?" Trevor asked with his mouth full.

"Yeah?" his mom responded as she wiped her hands and reached for her lit cigarette that was lying on the edge of the coffee cup.

"I want you to quit smoking."

His mom took a long drag on her cigarette and then slowly let the smoke blow out her nose.

"Why?" she wondered aloud. "Smoking is the only thing I really enjoy in life."

"Because it will kill you, Mom! I don't have a dad who cares, and I don't want to lose my mom. You can get help, you know—a patch or some gum or something."

"No, I'm too addicted," she said with a disgusted shake of her head.

"Mom, I know it's too difficult to do on your own. Go to the doctor and get help."

"I'll need more than a doctor's help to break this habit," she said as she dropped her cigarette into the half-filled coffee cup and walked out of the kitchen.

"Okay," Trevor mumbled to himself as he ripped off another bite of pizza. Then yelling through his mouthful, he said, "I'll ask Aaron to get God to help you. Aaron says his God can do anything!" But he figured his mom wasn't listening.

So we say with confidence,
"The Lord is my helper; I will not be afraid..."
Hebrews 13:6a

What About You?

Do you ask for help at the beginning of a task, or do you wait until it seems impossible before you ask God for help?

Like...

- Asking for help when you begin to study for a test?
- Asking for help as you practice and prepare for a game?
- Asking for help when you sense there is some tension between you and a friend?

Take Time to Pray!

Where do you need God's help? Ask God for help now before things get difficult.

Day 56

MY GOD IS HOLY

Read: Leviticus 19:2

Glenwood halls were spotted with a few straggling students as Aaron walked toward the school gym. His mother had a school committee meeting, so Aaron decided to wait around after school to get a ride home. He told his mom that when her meeting was finished, she could find him shooting hoops in the gym.

Aaron threw open the gym doors and was immediately stopped in his tracks at the sight of Jeremy, the skinny eighth-grade student who had made basketball tryouts miserable for Aaron.

"Hey, March, I watched you during the basketball season—you stunk. I don't know why you made the team." Jeremy sneered as he bounced the ball from hand to hand.

"At least, I made the team," Aaron responded without any expression.

Jeremy went for a layup and missed the basket. In disgust, he grabbed his gym bag and pushed open the side door. Aaron watched in silence, but Jeremy had one more thing to add before he left the gym. A string of cussing reverberated across the gym, letting Aaron know exactly what Jeremy thought of him; then the gym door shut, and Aaron was on his own.

Aaron bent down to pick up the basketball just as Coach Ryder's office door opened.

"Mr. March," Coach Ryder boomed, "I do not allow that kind of language in my gym, whether or not you missed a basket."

"Coach, that wasn't me," Aaron tried to explain.

Coach Ryder looked around the gym. "There's nobody else here, Mr. March. There's nobody else to blame." With these last words, Coach Ryder stepped back into his office and shut the door.

Aaron was furious with Jeremy; he was sure Jeremy knew the coach would be listening and would blame him for the cussing. Just then, the gym doors opened; and Aaron's mom poked in her head.

"Time to go, Aaron," she said with a smile.

Aaron was at a loss as he dropped the basketball, grabbed his backpack, and followed her to the car. Once they were on their way home, Aaron explained what had happened in the gym.

"Oh, Aaron, I'm sorry that happened," his mom sympathized, "but I don't think you should let this go. Coach Ryder needs to know that you serve a holy God, Who wants you to live a holy life—and that includes the words that come out of your mouth. You need to write the coach a letter explaining what happened and why you would never cuss like that. This could be an opportunity for you to share your faith with your coach. Don't worry, God will honor your honesty."

Aaron looked out the car window, thinking over what his mom had just said. A letter did seem to be the best way to handle the situation; and besides, he wanted the coach to know that he longed to be holy like God is holy.

> "'Be holy because I, the LORD your God, am holy.'"
>
> *Leviticus 19:2b*

What About You?

When people watch you, would they say you are holy like God is holy?

Like . . .

- When you stop yourself from saying a bad word?

- When you control your anger?

- When you choose to forgive and show kindness to someone who has been mean?

Take Time to Pray!

Chances are good that there have been times today when you have not been holy. Ask God to forgive you for those unholy times. Ask God to help you to be holy and thank God for being holy.

Day 57

MY GOD IS IMMORTAL

Read: I Timothy 1:17

For two weeks, Avery went faithfully to the barn every afternoon to check on and care for Rio. Finally, Avery felt Rio was ready to be lunged in the indoor arena. As Rio moved from a walk to a trot, she prayed for God's continued healing. Avery was hopeful that this Saturday morning, she would be able to get back in the saddle and ride Rio again.

Saturday finally arrived, and Avery's mom willingly drove her to the barn before 8:00 a.m. Avery was out of the car and into the barn before her mother opened her own car door.

As her mom walked into the barn, she overheard James saying to Avery, "Hey, I'm just a mere mortal. I didn't do anything to help Rio's healing process."

"I know. I'm just saying thank you," Avery explained as she slipped the halter over Rio's head.

James moved to the other end of the barn as Avery put Rio in the crossties.

"Mom," Avery whispered, "what does it mean to be a mere mortal?"

Avery's mom laughed and then leaned closer to explain, "It means you are human, not Divine. God is immortal because He has no human limitations. God's immortality is key to Who He is. If God wants to heal Rio, He can."

"And by the looks of things, He did," Avery said as she began to brush Rio. "I'm glad God isn't a mere mortal."

> *Now to the King eternal, immortal, invisible, the only God, be honor and glory for ever and ever. Amen.*
>
> I Timothy 1:17

What About You?

Are there times when you limit God because you forget He is immortal with no human limitations?

Like...

- When you figure He's not with you because you can't see Him?

- When you figure He's not listening because He doesn't answer you back verbally?

- When you figure He's not willing to forgive you because your friend won't forgive you?

Take Time to Pray!

Thank God for not having any limitations!

Day 58

MY GOD IS MY INTERCESSOR

Read: Romans 8:34

Kaylin wiped at her tears, blew her nose, then picked up the phone to call Avery.

"Hello?" Avery answered.

Kaylin's shaky voice replied, "Avery, it's me, Kaylin. I can't go to The Bridge's all-nighter because my parents don't get church and don't understand why I would want to spend all night with the church youth group."

"Oh, great," Avery said in annoyance. "Wait . . . do you think it would help if my mom spoke to your mom and explained the situation?"

"It couldn't hurt," Kaylin said hopefully.

"Let me call my mom." Avery pressed her phone against her stomach. "Mom, can you talk to Mrs. Wong about The Bridge's all-nighter?"

Avery's mom walked into the living room while drying her hands on a tea towel.

"You need an intercessor, do you?"

"No, Kaylin needs you to talk to her mom for her to explain why Kaylin should go."

Her mom laughed. "Avery, we're going to have to work on improving your vocabulary because that is exactly what an intercessor does—he talks to someone on another person's behalf."

"Okay, fine, will you be our intercessor?

"Gladly!" Avery's mom said as she took the phone from her daughter.

Ten minutes later, all was explained; and Kaylin was given permission to go. As her mom hung up the phone, she shared the good news with Avery and then added, "Avery, did you know that Jesus intercedes for us? Jesus sits beside God and talks to God about our salvation. He talks to God on our behalf."

"Cool!"

> *Christ Jesus . . .*
> *is at the right hand of God and is also interceding for us.*
> Romans 8:34b

What About You?

Knowing now that Jesus talks to God on your behalf, think of what would you like Jesus to say to God for you.

Like . . .

- You know that God gave you a good gift by sending Jesus to die for you.

- You are sorry for being a sinner that needed Jesus to die for you.

- You are glad Jesus rose from the dead and is representing you in Heaven.

Take Time to Pray!

Use the above ideas as a starting point for prayer. Thank God for interceding for you.

Day 59

MY GOD IS INVISIBLE

Read: I Timothy 1:17

"Hello, Ms. Bracken," Aaron said as he looked up from playing with Mickey. Realizing Trevor's mom needed some help, Aaron jumped up and bounded across the living room to grab some of the grocery bags from her hands.

"Here, let me take some of these to the kitchen for you," Aaron offered.

"Thanks, Aaron. Trev, you can get the rest of the bags out of the car."

"Ah, man." Trevor groaned as he pushed Mickey away and got to his feet. "Aaron, you make me look bad when you're so helpful."

Aaron ignored his friend's jab as he set the bags down on the kitchen table.

"Can I help you put any of these groceries away?"

"No thanks, Aaron. I need a break and a cigarette."

"I've been praying that you would quit," Aaron shared with raised eyebrows.

"Yeah, Trevor said he would ask you to do that. Your prayers aren't working yet," Ms. Bracken said as she lit her cigarette and leaned against the counter.

"Well, I'll just keep praying. By the way, I was wondering if Trevor could come to an all-nighter at my church this Saturday night? We play games and watch movies, and he might even get a little sleep. It's a lot of fun."

"Are you going to talk about that God you believe in—the One you can't even see?"

"Just because you can't see Him doesn't mean He's not real," Aaron defended. "We can't see Trevor right now, but we know he's around—"

"Hopefully getting the rest of the groceries," Ms. Bracken interjected.

"Yeah, and you can't see electricity, but you can see its power and its effect. That's just like God. You can't see Him, but you can see His power every day!"

Trevor stumbled into the kitchen, loaded with grocery bags, and deposited them all in the center of the floor.

"Well, the vanishing Trevor has appeared with the groceries; maybe your invisible God will appear to me, too," Ms. Bracken said sarcastically.

"God will reveal Himself; you just need to be watching," Aaron assured Ms. Bracken as he and Trevor returned to the living room to play with Mickey.

> Now to the King eternal, immortal, invisible,
> the only God, be honor and glory for ever and ever. Amen.
> I Timothy 1:17

What About You?

Where in creation do you see signs of your invisible God? Like...

- The hummingbirds and bees with their tiny wings that can support their big bodies?
- Tame animals that once were wild?
- The sun and rain working together to grow crops, so we can have food?

Take Time to Pray!

Share with God where you see Him at work in creation and how His work proves He is real.

Day 60

MY GOD IS JEALOUS

Read: Deuteronomy 4:23-24

The elevator door slid open as Avery stepped onto the plush carpet that covered Kaylin's apartment hallway. Avery felt like she was in the movies whenever she visited Kaylin's condominium; everything looked so rich and expensive.

Knowing that Kaylin was waiting, Avery pushed the doorbell and listened to the chimes that echoed through their vast two-story condo. The door flew open; then Kaylin, her hair pulled into a messy bun, turned and ran up the open staircase that led to the bedroom.

"Come on up, Avery," Kaylin called over her shoulder. "I'm at a critical point in putting on my makeup, and I can't stop to talk."

Avery laughed as she shut the door. Walking through the living room toward the stairs, Avery let her hand brush the back of the black leather couch. Her eyes drifted over the living room with the wall of windows that looked over the city. Suddenly, she noticed a statue on the coffee table. The statue sitting cross-legged with all sorts of arms doing odd things seemed ugly and out of place in the beautiful living room. Avery wondered why Kaylin's mom would waste her money on something so odd-looking.

Kaylin's call interrupted Avery's thoughts. "Are you coming up sometime today?"

"Yeah, yeah," Avery called as she bounded up the stairs and down the hallway to Kaylin's bathroom.

"Pull up a counter and make yourself comfortable," Kaylin mumbled as she put lip gloss on her lips. Moving aside the scattered makeup, Avery wiggled her way onto the counter and leaned against the mirror.

"Hey, what's up with that ugly statue stuck in the middle of your living room?"

"I don't know—my mom says it's a Buddhist goddess that was important to her grandmother, but those twenty-four arms kinda freak me out."

"She doesn't think it is a real goddess, does she?"

"You never know with my mom," Kaylin stated as she stood back from the mirror to survey her work.

"Do you think it looks good?"

"Ugly is more like it," Avery mused.

"Well, that's a nice thing to say about your best friend's new lip gloss!"

Avery gulped in a laugh, realizing what she had said. "No, Kaylin, I didn't mean you. I meant the statue. I just can't get it out of my mind. In the Bible, God deals harshly—I'm talking fire-from-Heaven kind of stuff—with those who worship idols."

"What's an idol?" questioned Kaylin as she brushed out her hair.

"My dad says it's anything that's more important to you than God. I guess that means you expect the idol to do things for you instead of trusting God for help." Avery shrugged as she finished her explanation.

"Well, that could be anything, not just the silly many-armed statue in my living room."

Avery flicked the blush brush across the counter as she said, "You mean like this stuff?"

Kaylin laughed.

"Are you implying that I'm expecting this makeup to work miracles?"

Avery rolled her eyes. "Remember, that was your thought, not mine. I don't want to get in trouble with my best friend. Besides, my mom is waiting for us down in the car. She wants to drop us off early for the all-nighter; so, get your stuff, and let's go!"

"Great, let me grab my bag," Kaylin said as she slipped into her bedroom.

For the LORD your God is a consuming fire, a jealous God.
Deuteronomy 4:24

What About You?

For us, jealousy is a sin but not for God. He deserves to receive all the honor and glory, and He doesn't like it when we praise or value something more than Him. Is there anything in your life that is more important to you than God?

Like...

- Friends?
- Sports?
- Money?

Take Time to Pray!

Tell God how much you value Him, how wonderful He is, and how He is worthy of all your praise.

Day 61
MY GOD IS JESUS

Read: John 10:30

Trevor and Aaron tossed their sleeping bags and pillows into the corner of the Sunday school classroom designated as the boy's sleeping room. From down the hall, they could hear Steve calling everybody to the youth room. There were over thirty junior high students at The Bridge for the all-nighter. It took Steve a couple of minutes to get them all settled.

"Here's the plan: we play games for the next hour. We take a food break—pizza and soda—and then we watch a movie. Let's begin the games! It's hide-and-seek in the dark with a twist. Avery, come on up here," Steve waved Avery forward.

Kaylin giggled at Avery as she went to stand beside Steve. He continued his explanation. "Avery will find a hiding spot. Then, with all the lights off in the church, we have to find her hiding spot. When you find her, you join her. The last person to find the group is 'it' next time."

Steve whispered in Avery's ear, "You better find a spot that can hold thirty kids." Then he nudged Avery on her way.

A few minutes later, the students began their search in the dark. The hide-and-seek game and pizza time were so much fun that it was nearly three hours later before the students were settling down with their pillows to watch the movie. Everyone quieted down as the opening credits for the movie began to play. The students were enjoying the movie. However, near the end, the main actor said "Jesus Christ," and it was clear he wasn't praying.

Aaron raised his eyebrow at Trevor, but Trevor just shrugged.

Steve hit pause on the remote and got up. He walked over and stood in front of the screen.

"I need everyone's attention before I resume playing the movie," Steve called. The students listened as Steve explained, "It's hard to find a movie with no cussing in it. I thought this movie would be a perfect choice. I didn't realize the actor used Jesus' name like that, and I'm sorry. I would have found something different for us to watch if I had known. However, this does provide an opportunity for me to explain that God takes His name very seriously. Would one of you look up Exodus 20:7?"

Avery quickly searched on her phone and then raised her hand when she found the verse. Steve asked her to read it out loud for the other students.

"You shall not misuse the name of the Lord your God, for the Lord will not hold anyone guiltless who misuses His name," Avery read.

"Thank you, Avery." Steve continued, "God's name is holy. We are to use His name respectfully and in prayer. Well, Jesus is God, and so His name is included in this command. Not only is the actor wrong for using Jesus' name this way, but we commit a sin when we do the same thing. I want you all to keep this in mind as we finish the movie. Afterwards, if anyone has any questions, I would be happy to talk more about this. But for now, enjoy the rest of the movie."

Trevor turned to Aaron with a frown.

"I hear Jesus' name being misused all the time. I didn't know it mattered."

"It matters!" Aaron said seriously as he pushed his pillow into place; then he settled down to finish watching the movie.

"I and the Father are one."

John 10:30

What About You?

Are there times when you slip into the world's way of misusing the Lord's name?

Like...

- Saying "Jesus" or "Jesus Christ" when you're trying to make a point?
- Saying God's name when you are surprised?
- Including "Lord" in a sentence for no reason?

Take Time to Pray!

Ask God to forgive you for the times you have misused His name. Ask God to help you to respect His name!

Day 62

MY GOD IS MY JUDGE

Read: II Timothy 4:8

Ms. Phillips droned on endlessly about fractions from the front of her class, oblivious to the note-passing that was taking place between the students. Kaylin nodded at Avery, who reached out and grabbed the note meant for Aaron. When Aaron finally got the note, he opened it and read, *I was distracted and didn't notice Jason Martinez. I wasn't trying to be mean by not saying hi.*

Aaron pulled out his pen and wrote back on the bottom of the note, *Seriously, you think you are better than him because you can walk, and he has to be in a wheelchair.*

When Kaylin read Aaron's note, she was so furious that she decided to yell at him after class rather than writing him back. Ms. Phillips finally finished her lecture on fractions, and the class was dismissed for the day.

Kaylin stormed up to Aaron at his locker and pushed his shoulder, forcing him to face her.

"How dare you judge my motives. I think Jason is great. Whether he is in a wheelchair or not does not matter to me. I didn't say hi to him because I was distracted."

"You know in your heart what the truth is," Aaron said with a shrug as he shoved his math book into his locker.

"Let God be my Judge, Aaron. You don't know enough about my heart to be my judge," Kaylin replied in disgust as she gave Aaron's shoulder another shove. Then, without further words, she went to her own locker.

> *The Lord, the righteous Judge...*
> *II Timothy 4:8*

What About You?

Do you judge other people's motives and actions instead of letting God be their Judge?

Like...

- When you watch the quiet new kid at school, and you think she's stuck up rather than shy?

- When you are bugged by a loudmouth team player, and you think he's obnoxious rather than motivated to win?

- When a classmate gets higher grades than you, and you figure she's been cheating rather than studying?

Take Time to Pray!

God is our fair, honest, and loving Judge. He knows what goes on in our hearts. Ask Him to forgive you for judging others. Thank Him for being a loving Judge of your heart.

Day 63
MY GOD IS JUST

Read: Deuteronomy 32:3-4

Kaylin slammed her locker shut as Avery came up behind her.

"Sill mad at Aaron?" Avery wondered.

"He thinks he can judge my motives. Yeah, you bet I'm still angry!" Kaylin fumed as she struggled to put her backpack on her back.

"Let it go, Kaylin. God is the Judge, and He'll serve justice. In the end, God makes sure the truth is seen—just like in the movies with those courtroom battles. God is fair; He knows the truth, and He will be the just Judge."

"What are you talking about?" Kaylin said with a screwed-up face. "I just want Aaron to know he's wrong."

"Then quit worrying about Aaron's words and take this opportunity to prove him wrong," Avery finished as she pointed at Jason wheeling down the hall.

Kaylin shut her locker and gave her full attention to Jason.

"Hi, Kaylin. Hi, Avery," Jason greeted them both.

"Hi, Jason!" they both said at the same time.

"Jason," Kaylin continued, "I am sorry if I missed saying hi to you this morning when you called to me in the parking lot. I was distracted; I didn't mean to be rude."

"No worries," Jason called over his shoulder with a smile on his face. "We're good, but I am late for class."

Kaylin glanced at Aaron's locker, but he was gone.

"Oh, I wish Aaron was still around to hear Jason's response; then he would judge my heart justly. "

"Justly?" Avery questioned as she tugged her in the direction of class.

"Yes, you know, like you said earlier, he would judge what is true."

I will proclaim the name of the LORD . . . all his ways are just.

Deuteronomy 32:3-4

What About You?

Are you quick to remind people that God is just and will make sure the truth is eventually seen?

Like . . .

- When you told the truth and were not believed?

- When you weren't involved in a wrongdoing, but everybody thought you were?

- When you had good motives, but your friends didn't think so?

Take Time to Pray!

Thank God for being a just God Who knows the truth and will help others to see that truth!

Day 64
MY GOD IS KIND

Read: Romans 2:1-4

Kaylin's phone began to vibrate in her back pocket as she struggled to unlock her apartment door. The vibrating stopped as she dropped her backpack onto the couch. Pulling out her phone, she saw that the caller had left a message.

A moment later, she heard, "Hey, Kaylin, I'm sorry. We need to talk. Can you call me?"

Kaylin plopped onto the couch as her call tried to connect.

"God, help me to do what is right during this call," she prayed.

"Hello?" Aaron answered.

"You wanted to talk?" Kaylin prodded.

"Yeah, I have been thinking about it, and I guess I could be wrong about how I judged your heart when you ignored Jason in the parking lot."

"You're right, Aaron!" Kaylin confirmed. "I was worried about the math test, and I wasn't really noticing anything around me."

"Well," Aaron explained, "Jason is a good guy, and I want everyone at school to see that."

Kaylin snapped back, "You think I could be one of those people who make fun of him because he gets around differently than we do?"

"Hey," Aaron interrupted, "I was trying to defend Jason, but I guess I got carried away and jumped to a conclusion about you."

"Yeah, it upsets me, too, when anyone is unkind to someone else just because someone is a bit different. I try to be kind to everyone, just like God is kind."

"Kaylin, that's wonderful, I wish all the students were like that. Oh, and will you forgive me for misjudging you?"

"Sure, Aaron."
"See you tomorrow?" Aaron asked.
"Okay, bye."

> *God's kindness is intended to lead you to repentance.*
> Romans 2:4b

What About You?

Do you recognize ways that God has shown His kindness to you? Like...

- Forgiving you every time you say you are sorry?
- Loving you even when you are mad at Him?
- Giving to you, even when you have a bad attitude?

Take Time to Pray!

Talk to God about His kindness to you, even when you don't deserve it.

Day 65
MY GOD IS KING

Read: Revelation 17:14

Trevor was scarfing down a bowl of popcorn while he and Aaron were watching the latest Wild Animal reels. Aaron rolled over and kicked at Trevor, hoping to move him further away.

"Man, can you get rid of those socks? They're killing the taste of the popcorn," groaned Aaron.

Trevor bent over his socks and took a big whiff.

"Ah! I guess you'll have to deal with it!"

Aaron gave up on the socks as a roar erupted from his phone. Both boys gagged as they watched the lion rip apart his newly captured dinner. Although neither boy wanted to admit it, they both had lost their appetite with the clip they had just witnessed. Aaron clicked off his phone as Trevor tugged at the Nerf ball poking out from underneath the couch.

"I guess all kings get to kill—even the king of the jungle, the lion," Trevor stated as he pushed to the end of the couch and threw the ball at Aaron. Trevor missed, but he managed to hit the bowl of popcorn and scatter it over the carpet. Aaron knew he would make Trevor clean it up later, but first, he had something he wanted to say.

"I know a King Who is kind, not a killer," Aaron announced.

"Yeah, well, if you're talking about the Busy Bee reel we watched last week, I don't think it counts because she's a queen, not a king!" Trevor was laughing at his own joke as he rolled off the couch and onto the popcorn-covered carpet.

Aaron flicked a kernel of popcorn at Trevor, hitting him on the end of his nose.

"Nah, I'm talking about the King of kings we read about in the Bible. I know Him personally, and He doesn't end life, He gives life." Aaron continued proudly, "At the end of time, everyone will see He is the King of kings, but, Trevor, it would be cool if you could see God as King right now."

Trevor wasn't in the mood for something so serious, but he did mumble, "Yeah, I'll think about it," as he began to pick up the popcorn.

The Lamb will triumph over them because he is Lord of lords and King of kings . . .

Revelation 17:14

What About You?

God wants to be the King of your life in every area. Is there an area of your life where you have made yourself king or queen, telling yourself what to do rather than letting God tell you what to do?

Like . . .

- Not letting your sister come into your room or borrow your things?

- Not forgiving a friend who has hurt you?

- Keeping your money for yourself, rather than giving some back to God?

Take Time to Pray!

Say sorry to God for wanting to be your own king or queen of your life. Ask God to help you let Him be the King in every area of your life.

Day 66

MY GOD IS LIFE-GIVING

Read: I Corinthians 15:45-47

Trevor got off his phone and turned to Aaron with a smile.

"My mom says I can go to The Bridge tonight just as long as I'm home by ten."

"Great, come on, my dad is waiting for us in the car," called Aaron as he turned toward the back door.

Trevor and Aaron were late arriving at the church, and the games had already begun. Steve had formed two groups. Each group received an extra-large set of coveralls they were to fill with their allotted balloons. The difference was that one team was blowing the air into the balloons they were stuffing in place and the other team was using a helium pump to blow up their balloons. The race was on!

Trevor and Aaron joined the helium team; and soon, their monster man was floating a few inches off the ground with the allotted balloons all stuffed into place. The helium team was the winner!

After the winners stopped their victory cheer, Steve had everyone sit in a semi-circle. He was flanked by the two balloon men as he began his talk.

"Balloon man to my left represents Adam, the first man on the earth. Adam made a bad choice; and as a result, *what* entered the world?" Steve waited for the answer to his *what* question.

Kaylin, sitting in the center of the semi-circle, quickly raised her hand. When Steve nodded at her, she called out "sin" with a big smile.

"Right," said Steve, "and the helium man to my right represents Jesus. He made a sacrificial choice to leave Heaven, to come to earth, and to die for us. Through faith in Jesus, we all can experience . . . " Steve looked around expectantly, wondering if anyone knew the right answer to finish his sentence.

Aaron, not wanting to be outdone by Kaylin, didn't bother to raise his hand but yelled out "salvation," knowing he was right.

"Excellent!" Steve said as he continued. "Jesus was the last Adam ending the reign of sin and death and giving us a chance at life. Helium man here," Steve tugged on the pant leg, making the balloon body bounce about in the air, "represents our Savior, Jesus. His death on the cross paid the penalty for our sins. We just need to say sorry for those sins and thank You to Jesus for what He has done for us through His death on the cross. Jesus wants to give us a great life here on earth, as well as eternal life in Heaven; we just need to respond to His gift. If you want to respond by saying sorry and thank You, then now is your chance." Steve bowed his head and began to pray.

As Steve prayed aloud, Aaron prayed silently for Trevor.

Please, God, it would be so excellent if Trevor finally said sorry and thank You to You.

> *So it is written: "The first man Adam became a living being"; the last Adam, a life-giving spirit.*
>
> *I Corinthians 15:45*

What About You?

Have you said sorry to God for having sinned and thank You to Jesus for dying on the cross and paying the penalty for those sins? Like . . .

- Lying, cheating, or dishonesty?

- Anger, impatience, or selfishness?

- Gossip, pride, or unforgiveness?

Take Time to Pray!

Now is a good time to say sorry and thank You to God if you have not already done so. If you have already thanked Jesus for His death on the cross to pay for your sins, then take this time to say sorry for the things you have done recently that you know make God sad. Also, pray for a friend you know who needs Jesus as his or her life-giving Savior.

Day 67
MY GOD IS LIGHT

Read: I John 1:5

Easter Sunday morning service began with a resurrection song sending chills down Avery's back. She loved being in church on Easter—a perfect place to celebrate Jesus' resurrection from the grave. The main part of the service was a dramatic presentation about Jesus' resurrection from the point of view of Mary Magdalene. Avery's sister, Sarah, was Mary Magdalene in the play. She was very convincing, and Avery felt chills again when Sarah announced, "Jesus said my name. With one word—*Mary*—my whole world changed. My Jesus is no longer dead; He is alive!"

At the end of the dramatic presentation, their pastor came to the pulpit and read the words of John 1:5: "The light shines in the darkness, and the darkness has not overcome it." As the pastor read these words, the clouds from outside moved; and the sunlight streamed in the windows, bathing the congregation in light.

"Friends," the pastor said, "Jesus came to earth to be the Light, allowing us to see the truth. Many people did not understand His truth, and they crucified Him. However, Jesus' death is part of God's plan. Jesus needed to die for our sins, but only Jesus, God's Son, could have risen again. Mary Magdalene was right; He is alive! Jesus' truth remains the same today. Jesus is our risen Savior, the Light of the world."

As the pastor prayed out loud, Avery felt the warmth of the sun streaming in on her. Avery prayed silently, *Thank You, God, for being the Light of the world and for sending Jesus to be my Savior!*

God is light...
I John 1:5

What About You?

Do you let Jesus' light—the light that reveals truth—shine into the dark places in your life?

Like...

- Your secret, sinful thoughts?
- Your poor attitude toward your parents?
- Your selfish plans?

Take Time to Pray!

Ask God to shine His light into the dark places in your life; and then ask Him to help you change those thoughts, attitudes, and actions that don't please Him.

Day 68

MY GOD LIVES

Read: Galatians 2:20

Trevor sat proudly beside his mother at the Easter service. He was so glad that Aaron's family had invited them to the Sunday service and then over for lunch. The pastor said his final prayer, and then the service was dismissed. Aaron, who was sitting on the other side of Trevor, nudged him.

"Hey, look, there are Avery and Kaylin."

Just as Aaron said this, Avery noticed the two guys and waved. Trevor was torn. He didn't want to leave his mom on her own, but he wanted to go over and say hi to the girls.

This choice was taken from him when Mrs. March said, "Trevor, we are heading home right away. The roast will be burned if I don't get it out of the oven. You and your mom can follow us home in your car. I'm sure Aaron will ride with you to keep you company."

Trevor nodded; and then, they filed out of the row and down the aisle to the back of the church.

On their way home, Aaron asked Trevor's mom some questions concerning the service. "Ms. Bracken, did you like the dramatic presentation?"

"Yes," she said with an unusual smile. "Avery's sister was very convincing."

"Did you like the part about Jesus being raised?" Aaron wondered.

Trevor's mom screwed up her face and then rubbed her nose awkwardly as she turned her car onto Aaron's street.

"Aaron, honestly, I have trouble believing God is alive—not to mention the fact that Jesus lives. I know it's a fact for you and your family, but God seems more dead than alive to me."

"Oh, He lives, Ms. Bracken; just think of what a mess this world would be in if God was dead!"

Christ lives in me . . .
Galatians 2:20

What About You?

How would your world be different if God were dead? *Like . . .*

- The bullies at school make all the rules?
- People are free to come into your house and take your stuff?
- There is no beauty in the world?

Take Time to Pray!

Thank God that He lives, that Jesus lives, and that you have life.

Day 69
MY GOD IS LORD

Read: Nehemiah 9:6

Curled up on her swinging chair with her blue comforter pulled around her, Kaylin was enjoying reading her latest novel. *Vince's Victory* was the second novel in a new mystery series Kaylin had found at the library.

For Kaylin, the quiet Saturday stretched out in front of her as she found herself lost in the story of Vince, the fourteen-year-old son of Lord Vancheska. The Vancheskas lived in a castle surrounded by a moat. Vince loved to ride his horse, Splendor; to shoot apples out of the top of a tree with his bow and arrow; and best of all in Kaylin's mind, to solve mysteries with the insights he got from his dad.

Kaylin took a reading break to grab a handful of popcorn. A piece of popcorn caught in her throat, resulting in a coughing fit. Dropping her book, Kaylin ran to her bathroom, cupped some cold water in her hands, and began sipping the water. Once Kaylin recovered from the coughing fit, she took a moment to study herself in the mirror.

I wonder what it would be like to be the son of a lord, Kaylin thought as she pulled her hair back into a ponytail. *Living in a castle and having a dad who rode with you, shot arrows with you, and solved mysteries with you—that would be so cool.*

Suddenly, a new thought struck Kaylin, and she started to giggle.

"Wait a minute," she said aloud, "I'm a daughter of a Lord—actually, *the* Lord; and He is always with me, showing me cool stuff."

With that new thought, Kaylin smiled heavenward and winked at her Lord.

"Thanks for letting me be Your daughter!" she prayed out loud. Then sighing, she left the bathroom to return to her book.

> *You alone are the LORD...*
> *Nehemiah 9:6a*

What About You?

Have you ever thought about all the cool stuff you get to see and the insight you have because you are the child of the Lord?

Like...

- Seeing a sunset and knowing God painted it?

- Hearing the roar of a lion at the zoo and knowing God can tame it?

- Getting a new haircut and realizing God knows how many hairs are on your head?

Take Time to Pray!

Let God know that you are glad He is the Lord of your life. Thank Him for the benefits you experience because you are His child.

Day 70

MY GOD IS MAJESTIC

Read: Exodus 15:11

Spring was finally here, and Trevor and Aaron planned to spend all of Saturday outdoors. The two guys met in front of Glenwood on their bikes, each balancing their fishing poles and tackle boxes on their handlebars. Their destination was the forest that bordered Bell Line Road. They stopped at the convenience store for a cold soda to add to their packed lunch before continuing.

Trevor entered the dirt path first, with Aaron close behind. They followed the winding forest trail to the stream, where they were soon settled with their hooks dangling in the water.

"I told my mom I was bringing home supper," Trevor bragged.

"Bet you I get the biggest catch," Aaron countered.

"You're on! The loser has to share his dessert with the winner. I have sweet cakes; what do you have?" Trevor asked.

"My mom's homemade chocolate chip cookies," Aaron said with a proud smile.

Trevor didn't get a chance to respond as his line tugged, and he reeled in a beautiful bass.

It took Aaron another hour before his line began to whirl.

"It's a big one!" Aaron yelled as Trevor dropped his rod and grabbed the net, ready to help his friend. For five minutes, Aaron fought with his catch, trying desperately not to break his line. In a last-ditch effort to escape, the fish jumped from the water; but Trevor caught it with the net.

"Wow, what an awesome fish!" Trevor said in amazement.

"Majestic is more like it. I wish I had my camera. I've never seen such an amazingly big and beautiful fish come out of this river," Aaron said. Then, raising one eyebrow, he added, "Boy, your sweet cakes are sure going to taste good!"

> *Who among the gods is like you, LORD? Who is like you—majestic in holiness, awesome in glory, working wonders?*
>
> *Exodus 15:11*

What About You?

What would you use to describe God's majesty?
Like...

- A king on a throne in his royal robes?
- An awesome sunrise full of bold colors that fill the sky?
- A powerful, roaring waterfall?

Take Time to Pray!

Share with God where you best see His majesty displayed.

Day 71

MY GOD IS MARVELOUS

Read: Revelation 15:3

The back door flew open with a bang. Aaron's mom turned in surprise to see him standing in the doorway with a huge smile spread across his face.

"Well, the fisherman comes home," Aaron's mom cooed.

"Proud fisherman, you mean—wait 'til you see my catch," Aaron said as he strode over to the sink and unloaded his majestic fish.

"Wow, Aaron, that is one marvelous fish!"

"I think it will feed our whole family!" Aaron enthused. "I'll clean it, Mom, if you would be willing to fry it for supper."

His mom agreed as he made his way to the backyard with a bucket and a knife. Aaron had watched his father clean fish before, and he was sure he was up for the task. However, a few grunts and exclamations later, it was apparent that Aaron needed the help of his dad.

"You're well on your way to having that marvelous fish ready for dinner; but if we don't want to chew on scales and crunch on a few bones, I better step in and help," Aaron's dad offered. An hour later, the four sat down at the dinner table, the smell of fried fish filling the air.

"Aaron," his dad declared, "I am marveling that this fish came from Bell Line River. It is a wonder it lasted so long without being caught. I'm at a loss for words, except to say it's marvelous, and I'm glad we get to eat it for dinner."

Then Aaron's dad bowed his head and prayed. What followed was a fun dinner where all enjoyed Aaron's marvelous fish.

Great and marvelous are your deeds, Lord God Almighty...
Revelations 15:3

What About You?

You marvel at many things in your life, but how often do you marvel at God? Consider some of the things you marvel at.
Like...

- The speed of a cheetah.
- The powerful jaws of a crocodile catching its prey.
- A concert pianist whose fingers race up and down the keyboard while playing a beautiful melody.

Take Time to Pray!

Have you ever marveled at Who God is? Have you ever listed the marvelous things God does that make your mouth drop open in amazement? Share that list with God now.

Day 72

MY GOD IS MERCIFUL

Read: Luke 6:36

Trevor walked through his front door, exhausted from a long day at school. Dropping his backpack on the living room chair, he rubbed his eyes with a sigh. A cold soda and his favorite TV show were just what he needed. He dragged himself to the kitchen in search of the soda when he was stopped in his tracks by a mess that covered the floor.

"Mickey," Trevor growled, "you are in a lot of trouble!"

The garbage bag left at the back door was ripped open, and the contents were spread over the entire kitchen floor. Furious, Trevor went in search of his puppy. He found Mickey on his mother's bedspread chewing a steak bone. Trevor grabbed Mickey by the scruff of the neck and pulled him to the floor. Mickey planted his hindquarters and dug in with his back paws, unwilling to visit the kitchen mess, but Trevor was not going to allow Mickey to win. The next hour was filled with Trevor's complaints as he cleaned up the mess.

When Trevor's mom arrived home, the mess was completely cleaned up, except for the stain left by the steak bone on his mom's bedspread. It only took Trevor's mom one minute alone in her bedroom to notice the stain and start to yell.

"Trevor, get in here!" she bellowed.

"Yeah, Mom?" Trevor asked as he stood in her doorway.

"What's this?" His mom pointed to the stain.

"Mickey got a steak bone and decided to enjoy it on your bed," Trevor answered sheepishly.

"What?" Trevor's mom exploded, "That's it! That puppy is out of here. He's gone. Go get that mutt. We're taking him to the pound."

Trevor turned on his heels and ran down the hall to his room. He needed help. Quickly, he called Aaron and explained the situation to him. Aaron's response was simple.

"Trev, I'm going to pray. What you and Mickey need is some mercy. I'll pray right now that you don't receive what you deserve. Mickey deserves to go to the pound according to your mom, but I'm going to pray that doesn't happen."

Just as Aaron finished his prayer, Trevor's door opened, and his mom stuck in her head.

"I'll give you fifteen minutes to clean up that stain. If you can get rid of the stain, Mickey can stay."

"Did you hear that, Aaron?" Trevor whispered into the phone.

"That's mercy, Trev. Call me back in fifteen minutes, and let me know what happens."

Fifteen minutes later, Trevor was sharing with Aaron the good news that Mickey was staying.

> *Be merciful, just as your Father is merciful.*
> *Luke 6:36*

What About You?

If mercy is not receiving what you deserve, then can you identify times when you have received mercy?

Like...

- When you got a stain on your sister's shirt, and she forgave you rather than making you buy her a new shirt?
- When you received money for doing a job, even though you complained the whole time you did the job?

- When you deserved to be grounded, and your parents let you go to the movies, anyway?

Take Time to Pray!

Thank God for His mercy in your life and ask Him to help you to show mercy to others.

Day 73
MY GOD IS A MYSTERY

Read: Job 11:7-9

Excitement rippled through the science class as Mr. Pritchard announced the beginning of the mystery segment. Kaylin was especially happy because Avery was her partner. The two girls had chosen to research, prepare, and present "The Mystery of Migration."

As Avery was logging in, Kaylin sat back in her chair and wondered aloud, "We're probably not going to get an A on this project, you know. It is impossible to solve the mystery of how these birds know when to leave, where to go, and when to return."

Avery laughed to herself. "Kaylin, Mr. Pritchard wants us to present the mysteries, not solve them. There are some mysteries we'll never solve—well, here on earth, anyway."

"Speaking of mysteries, there is one big mystery I've been trying to figure out about God," Kaylin mused.

"Only one?" interrupted Avery.

"No, it's just the one for this week," admitted Kaylin.

"Yeah, what's that?" asked Avery.

"God was never born, and He will never die—no beginning or end. How can that be?" Kaylin dropped her voice to a whisper as Mr. Pritchard gave them the eye from across the classroom.

Avery took a break from typing and turned to answer her friend. "There are things about God we'll never understand; and in a way, I'm kind of glad. If we could completely figure Him out, then that would make Him like me; God is too big for that. When we get to Heaven, the mysteries about God will be solved; and that's enough for me."

"So, I guess I will have to wait for Heaven to get that question answered." Kaylin sighed as she tucked her black hair behind her ears. She leaned forward and focused on the computer screen while she whispered, "Well, here on earth, at least we can see what the internet has to say about migration; and maybe we can understand that a bit better."

> *"Can you fathom the mysteries of God..."*
> *Job 11:7*

What About You?

What are some of the mysteries about God that you don't understand?

Like...

- How He can hear everyone's prayers at the same time?
- The Trinity has three parts that make up one God?
- The fact that He loves us even when we do things wrong?

Take Time to Pray!

Thank God that one day in Heaven, your mysteries about Him will be solved.

Day 74
MY GOD IS PATIENT

Read: II Peter 3:15

"Come on, Aaron; I'm asking for fifteen minutes," Justin whined as he stood in front of the TV.

"Fine," Aaron fumed, "get our gloves, bat, and ball from the garage; and I'll meet you in the backyard in a minute."

Justin raced for the garage as Aaron slowly got up from the couch and flicked off the TV. Aaron found Justin in the backyard, already crouched in a batting position.

"Not too fast, okay, Aaron?" Justin called to his older brother.

Aaron nodded as he picked up his glove and worked the ball around in his hand.

"Okay, try to hit this, Justin," Aaron said as he let a pitch fly.

Justin swung and missed.

"I said slow! Cut it out, Aaron! You know I can't hit your fastball."

"Yeah, well, I'm trying to get this over as quickly as possible. So, get your bat up and concentrate."

The next ten minutes were filled with Aaron's fast pitches, Justin's swinging and missing, and Aaron's frustrated comments.

"What a waste of time," Aaron complained as Justin tossed the softball back to him. In frustration, Justin began to cry; and this just made Aaron angrier.

Just then, the back door opened.

"Aaron!" his mother called.

"Yeah?" Aaron responded.

"Come here," she commanded.

Aaron threw down his ball and glove and strode over to the back door.

"You're not being very patient with Justin," their mom observed.

"He's not keeping his eye on the ball, and he's not trying," Aaron shot back.

"I wonder if that's what God would say about you sometimes—that you're not trying? Yet God is patient with you. Be patient with Justin. Slow the ball down. When Justin gets a dozen good hits, you can come in."

"A dozen?" Aaron was horrified, "I'll be out here all night!"

"You only need to be a few more minutes if you just patiently work with him."

Our Lord's patience means salvation . . .
II Peter 3:15

What About You?

Are you as patient with other people as God is patient with you? Like . . .

- Talking gently when you are frustrated with a friend who is taking too long?
- Waiting quietly when you wish your parents would hurry?
- Finishing a difficult task without yelling or complaining?

Take Time to Pray!

Thank God for being patient with you as you learn to obey Him. Ask Him to help you to be patient with others.

Day 75

MY GOD IS MY PEACE

Read: Isaiah 9:6

Aaron's dad flicked off the TV. "Spring is here, son, and it is time to add mowing the lawn to your Saturday chores."

Aaron groaned as he rolled off the couch. "Why am I the only kid who has to spend Saturday mowing the lawn?"

"Let's see if we can do it without complaining," his dad challenged.

"Let's see if I have energy left to do anything else once I'm done," Aaron added sarcastically as he dragged his feet toward the back door.

The next ten minutes just added to Aaron's frustration. The lawn mower needed gas. While Aaron was filling the lawn mower, gas spilled over his pant leg. After changing his pants and pulling on a new pair of sneakers, Aaron caught his finger in the back door on his way out. Then, to top it all off, he had to move Justin's bike and rollerblades out of the way before he could get the lawn mower out of the garage.

Within the hour, Aaron finished his job, but his mood was not any better.

"Aaron?" Dad called as he came around the corner.

"What do you want now, Dad?"

"Well, I was going to take you to the bike shop to get that part for your bike, but I won't be taking you when you are in such a bad mood."

Still grumbling, Aaron pushed the lawn mower into the garage. "You can't blame me, Dad, 'cause everything has gone wrong."

"Son, that's where prayer and the peace of God come into play. Did you pray and ask God for His peace in the struggles?"

"No!"

"As you climb into the car, ask God to calm your spirit and bring you peace. His peace is a precious gift, and He'll give it to you if you just ask."

> *And he will be called . . . Prince of Peace.*
> *Isaiah 9:6*

What About You?

Can you think of times when you were upset over a difficult situation and did not handle it in a way that honored God?

Like . . .

- Yelling when things fall apart?
- Complaining when things are difficult?
- Getting angry when you don't get your way?

Take Time to Pray!

Ask God to help you stop, take a deep breath, and then pray for peace when you find yourself in a difficult situation.

Day 76
MY GOD IS PERFECT

Read: Matthew 5:48

Kaylin and Avery slid into place at the lunchroom table; each girl had a chicken burger, fries, and milk on their tray. Kaylin grabbed a French fry and began to chew.

"This is a perfect lunch," Avery mused as she picked up her chicken burger and took a big bite.

"No, the word *perfect* can only be applied to Carlos Lopez," Kaylin corrected.

"Seriously," Avery said as she slammed her chicken burger onto her plate, "Carlos is not perfect!"

"What is your problem?" Kaylin looked confused.

"Lately, you have been talking way too much about boys. Kaylin, Carlos is in eighth grade, and he is not interested in getting a girlfriend. He only wants to play football. Yeah, he is cute, but he is far from perfect."

"A girl can dream," Kaylin mused as she shoved another French fry into her mouth.

"Hey, Kaylin, maybe you could do something better than dreaming about boys," Avery said as she opened her milk and took a long sip. "Why don't you try praying for them? What do you think Carlos would like you to pray for him?"

"I don't know. Maybe that his throwing arm would improve, so he can make the team when he goes to high school."

"Yes," Avery said with raised eyebrows and a sly smile. "See, Carlos is not perfect, and I think he would appreciate a prayer more than a silly grin from across the gym."

Kaylin choked in laughter as she quickly grabbed her milk to help wash down the French fry.

> *Be perfect, therefore, as your heavenly Father is perfect.*
> *Matthew 5:48*

What About You?

Here on earth, we are to strive to be perfect, but only God is perfect. Have you ever stopped and really thought about how perfect God is?

Like . . .

- How perfect He is in all He says in the Bible?
- How perfect He is in His plans for you?
- How perfect He is without any human flaws?

Take Time to Pray!

God is perfect, and He knows it; but He likes you to share with Him how glad you are that you have a perfect God, so tell Him!

Day 77

MY GOD IS PRESENT

Read: Deuteronomy 31:8

Kaylin rushed down her stairs, frightened by the alarm sounding through her high-rise apartment building. She pushed the button on the front door intercom, and a recorded message blasted through the speaker. *There is an intruder in the building. He may be armed and dangerous. Don't open your front door. Remain in your apartment until further notice.*

Kaylin scrambled for her phone and called her mother—no answer. Then she tried to contact her father—no answer. A frustrated tear sprang from her eye as she threw her phone onto the couch.

"Why are they never around? Why don't they care? Why am I all alone with a crazy man in the building looking for who-knows-what?" she cried out to an empty room.

Kaylin didn't want to leave the living room, just in case another message came through the intercom. So, grabbing a fluffy gray throw, she wrapped the blanket around herself as she snuggled into the corner of the couch. She wanted to hurl something at the silly statue of the goddess, who was supposed to be protection for their house.

With the alarm still ringing in her ear, she dropped her head onto the leather arm of the couch and began to pray.

God, in Your Word, You promise to never leave us, to always be with us, to protect us. Right now, I am so glad You are here with me. I would be losing my mind if all I had to protect me was that silly goddess. Thanks for never leaving me, amen.

As Kaylin said the amen, the alarm stopped ringing. She lurched from the couch and pressed the intercom button. She leaned her head against the wall as she listened to the recording a second time. *The man has been caught. The police are here. The building is secure. You are safe to leave your apartment. The threat is over.*

Kaylin smiled and breathed a prayer of thanks to God.

> *"The LORD himself goes before you and will be with you;*
> *he will never leave you nor forsake you.*
> *Do not be afraid; do not be discouraged."*
>
> Deuteronomy 31:8

What About You?

Do you take comfort in knowing that God is always with you? He is omnipresent, which means always present. This should bring you comfort.

Like...

- When you are feeling lonely.
- When you need some support or encouragement.
- When you need someone to care.

Take Time to Pray!

Thank God for never leaving you, for always being present in your life. Thank God that you never have to be afraid or discouraged because He is always with you.

Day 78

MY GOD IS MY PROVIDER

Read: Genesis 22:14

The small red ball bounced across the living room floor, sending Mickey running after his prized toy. Trevor laughed at his dog as Mickey retreated down the hall, his ball clamped firmly between his teeth.

"Mickey doesn't seem to want to play anymore," Trevor's mom observed as she emerged from the hall into the living room.

"Nah, he's grumpy; he doesn't want to share," Trevor explained.

"Speaking of grumpy, I might be a little grumpy over the next few weeks."

"So, what's new? You are always grumpy," Trevor quipped.

"Hey, I'm trying to talk seriously to you for a minute. Could you cut it with the sarcasm?" his mom asked as she dropped into the living room chair.

"Okay, what's going to make you grumpy?" Trevor pulled himself onto the couch and faced his mom.

Rolling up her sleeve, she revealed a patch on her arm. "I went to the doctor's office and got some help to quit smoking."

"That patch will make a difference?" Trevor wondered.

"It will provide me with enough nicotine so that I can stop the cigarettes; and soon, I should be able to stop wearing the patch, too."

"Wow, Mom! I'll put up with your grumpy moods if you can stick to the doctor's plan."

"It's a deal," Trevor's mom said with a smile.

"Hey," Trevor erupted from the couch, "I have to call Aaron with the good news."

A few minutes later, Trevor was sharing the doctor's plan with Aaron. Aaron laughed. "Great news, Trev. Like Steve, our youth pastor says, 'You pray, and God will provide a way!'"

The LORD Will Provide . . .
Genesis 22:14

What About You?

As you pray for specific issues in your life, do you continue to pray faithfully as you watch to see how God will provide?

Like . . .

- Praying for enough money to purchase something you need, then working hard to earn it?

- Praying for a friend or family member to become a Christian, then sharing your faith with them?

- Praying for help to do well on a test, then working with God to study as hard as you can?

Take Time to Pray!

Review your list of specific prayer requests you have been bringing before God. Let God know you will continue to pray for these items while you watch to see how He will provide.

Day 79
MY GOD IS MY REALITY

Read: Colossians 2:17

The smell of cut grass was in the air as Kaylin ran down the sidewalk, trying to catch up to Aaron.

"Hey, slow down!" Kaylin called to Aaron. "You didn't waste any time getting out of school. Do you have a homework emergency you're rushing home to take care of?" Kaylin laughed at her own joke.

Aaron scowled in response.

"Kaylin, you don't normally walk this way. What's up?"

"Avery keeps bugging me, making me think I don't stand a chance with Carlos."

"You don't! Get over it!" Aaron gruffly replied.

"Oh, nice. You, too?"

"Avery says you're crazy to even think you stand a chance with Carlos, and I agree."

"Oh great, what else did Avery say?" Kaylin wondered as she repositioned her backpack.

"Lately, Avery has a lot to say. Every time you walk away, Avery has some kind of snide remark about the 'Carlos situation.' Forget Avery. I think you need to face reality. Look at what God has given you that is a part of your real life, not a part of your imagination."

"You mean, like you and Trevor?" Kaylin mumbled.

"Hey, don't get any ideas," Aaron said as he moved to the other side of the sidewalk. "God has given you a great reality with an amazing condo, lots of money, great friends, a new church, and a good relationship with Him. The best part is God, Kaylin! He is at the center of your reality."

"Hmm," Kaylin mused with a shrug. "I'll think about it."

With that, she turned and walked in the direction of her condo.

The reality, however, is found in Christ.
Colossians 2:17b

What About You?

Do you spend more time focusing on the things you dream of in your imagination than you do thanking God for the reality He has given you?

Like...

- Longing for a game you will purchase and conquer, rather than enjoying all the games you have that God has given to you already?

- Wanting a better set of friends, rather than seeing that God has given you friends you can influence to know and love God more?

- Hoping to move to someplace better, rather than appreciating what God has given you right now?

Take Time to Pray!

Thank God for being the Center of your reality. Thank Him for five specific *real* things in your life.

Day 80
MY GOD IS RECONCILING

Read: II Corinthians 5:18-19

Once Aaron got home from school, he went straight to his room. Flopping onto his bed, he stared at the ceiling.

"God, I think I messed up again. I said too much to Kaylin about Avery. I exaggerated to make my point, actually. I lied, and I am sorry for that. I know Kaylin is mad at Avery, and I didn't help the situation. What should I do?"

While Aaron was praying, a few blocks away, Kaylin was slamming her front door. During her walk home, her anger toward Avery continued to grow. By the time Kaylin jumped onto her couch with her phone in her hand, she was ready to give Avery an earful.

"Hello," Avery answered the call.

"Yeah, it's your so-called best friend. Aaron just told me how you've been talking behind my back."

"About what?"

"Don't play innocent! About Carlos, of course." Kaylin's screen flashed Aaron's interrupting call. "Hey, Aaron's calling."

"Good, I don't think I like the way this conversation is going." Avery hung up.

Kaylin clicked on Aaron's call.

"Kaylin, I'm sorry. Avery really didn't say all those things. Actually, I think she only made a comment once, and that was to say you should be praying for Carlos rather than trying to flirt with Carlos."

"Great timing, Aaron. Avery just hung up on me."

"Do you want me to call her and set things straight?" Aaron wondered.

"That would help," Kaylin acknowledged.

Two minutes later, the phone rang; and Kaylin grabbed it.

"Hello?" Kaylin answered.

"Hey, it's your so-called best friend," Avery said.

"Do you forgive me?" Kaylin wondered.

"Yeah, Aaron set it straight. At least, he was willing to go between us and make it right," Avery offered, "even if he did exaggerate in the first place."

> *God was reconciling the world to Himself in Christ...*
> *II Corinthians 5:19*

What About You?

Jesus has the ministry of reconciliation, which means He goes between God and us and makes sure things are right between us. He doesn't have to apologize for any mistakes like Aaron did. Instead, He represents the truth—the redemption that comes from His death on the cross. Jesus is great at reconciling things between God and us, but how are you at doing that with others?

Like...

- Helping to keep the peace between your brothers and sisters?

- Bringing clarity to confusing conversations between your friends?

- Helping your brother or sister see that your parents want what is best for them?

Take Time to Pray!

Thank Jesus for reconciling us to God. Ask God to help you to know what to say when you need to encourage reconciliation between your family members or friends.

Day 81

MY GOD IS MY REDEEMER

Read: Ephesians 1:7

The rain fell hard on Kaylin and Avery as they dashed from the car into the mall. The crowds inside the mall were proof that the rain would continue all day. There was nothing better to do than to go shopping.

Kaylin and Avery didn't waste any time; they went straight to their favorite store, Dingle Dangle.

"Hey, Kaylin, I should get this cool hair clip to help keep this mess off my face," Avery said.

Kaylin laughed at her friend's hair plastered against her face.

"I can't look at the hair clips," Kaylin explained. "I have a coupon to redeem for a pair of earrings."

"You are planning on paying for the earrings this time?" Avery teased.

"Avery." Kaylin looked upset. "We had a deal that you wouldn't mention my stealing again."

"I'm sorry," Avery said with a shrug. "It was so long ago, and you learned your lesson; so, I thought I could tease you about it. Forget what I said, okay? Now, let me see this coupon."

Kaylin pulled the coupon out of her pocket. It read, *Redeem this coupon at Dingle Dangle—buy one, get one free.*

"With this coupon, I can get that second pair of earrings; and nobody has to pay."

"Kaylin, the word *redeem* means "paid with a price." It's just that the store is willing to pay the price, so you don't have to."

"Well, however you want to explain it, it means I get a second pair of earrings," Kaylin said with a big grin as she spun the rotating display of earrings.

> *In him we have redemption through his blood,*
> *the forgiveness of sins...*
>
> *Ephesians 1:7a*

What About You?

Jesus redeemed you; He paid the price so you could get into Heaven free. The price He paid was dying on the cross. Jesus also paid the price to free you from many things here on earth.

Like...

- Feeling depressed.
- Feeling ashamed.
- Feeling hopeless.

Take Time to Pray!

Thank Jesus for paying the price for your sins. Thank Him for shedding His blood on the cross so that He could redeem you.

Day 82

MY GOD IS MY REFUGE

Read: Psalm 46:1

Avery sat curled up on the living room couch as her parents paced in front of their big bay window. The rain had continued to pour all day, while the storm seemed to get stronger. Avery pulled a blanket over her shoulders, feeling the need for some sort of comfort. She knew her parents' concern for Sarah was real. Her sister, Sarah, had only been driving for two months.

Their dad handed over the keys at lunch with the words, "Sarah, you make sure you're home before dark."

It was now 9:00 p.m., and the sun had set several hours earlier. No phone call and no Sarah. No one seemed to want to talk about the "what if's" that were racing through Avery's mind.

Suddenly, the phone buzzed, making everybody in the room jump. Avery's dad grabbed his phone from the coffee table. Avery moved to her knees, wanting to be closer, hoping for good news.

"Dad, is it Sarah? Is she all right?"

Her dad motioned for silence as the color drained from his face and his hands began to shake. He groaned as he spoke into the phone, "We'll be right there."

Avery's mom began to cry as Avery's dad explained that Sarah had been in a car accident and had been taken by ambulance to the hospital. Sarah was in bad shape, and the hospital needed a parent's okay before they could operate.

Avery watched through the sheet of rain as the car slipped down the driveway and slowly made its way down their street. She went over to Riley, who was sitting on the couch, and dropped down beside her.

"I think we need to pray," Avery whispered.

God is our refuge and strength, an ever-present help in trouble.
Psalm 46:1

What About You?

Can you think of ways God helps you when you are in trouble? Like...

- Sending someone to help you?
- Giving you peace as you pray to Him?
- Helping you find a verse in the Bible that will show you what He wants you to do?

Take Time to Pray!

Ask God to help you learn to turn to Him and find strength in Him every time you feel trouble pressing in around you.

Day 83

MY GOD IS MY REST

Read: Joshua 21:44

It wasn't until the early morning hours that Avery's dad came home from the hospital. Avery sat up in bed when she realized it was her dad walking down the hall. "Dad?"

"Yeah, honey?" Dad stuck his head into Avery's bedroom.

"How is Sarah?"

"She'll be fine. The operation was a success. They stopped the bleeding."

"Oh, good!" Avery said with a sigh. "Where's Mom?"

"She stayed with Sarah at the hospital. I've come home to get some rest. You need to do the same, so go back to sleep." Dad started to leave.

"Dad?"

"Yeah?" Dad stuck his head in once again.

"How do you get some rest when you are so worried? I've had a hard time sleeping."

Dad came in and sat down on the bed beside Avery.

"Well, honey, I guess the first thing I do to rest in God is to recognize that He will bring peace to my heart, the kind of peace that no one else can. Tonight, I had to leave the outcome of the surgery and Sarah's health in God's care. He can look after Sarah much better than I ever could. Now, I will go to sleep; and I want you to rest in God, too, so you can sleep."

Avery's dad tucked her back into bed and gave her a kiss on the forehead. After a short prayer, Avery felt ready to really sleep.

> *The LORD gave them rest...*
>
> *Joshua 21:44a*

What About You?

Are there times in your life when you find it difficult to rest—to trust and relax—in God?

Like...

- When a friend or family member gets hurt, and you don't know what to do to help them get better?

- When you try out for a team, and you must wait to see if you've made it?

- When you take an important test, and you won't find out your score for a week?

Take Time to Pray!

Ask God to help you to learn to rest in His care during times when you would naturally worry.

Day 84

MY GOD IS RIGHTEOUS

Read: Psalm 11:7

The following few days after Sarah's accident were serious ones in the McPherson household. Friday afternoon, almost a week later, Sarah came home from the hospital. The doctors said she needed another week of bed rest, and then she could go back to school. It was difficult for Avery to see her older sister in pain as she lay in her bed, propped up by several pillows.

"Sarah?" Avery whispered as she tiptoed into her sister's room. Sarah opened her eyes and stared back at Avery. "Does it hurt a lot?"

"Only when I have to answer my sister's questions," Sarah mumbled.

"You must be getting better if you have enough energy to have an attitude," Avery said as she sat down on Sarah's bed. "This isn't right, the way you got hurt. I'm mad at God because He let it happen."

Sarah's eyes widened as she struggled to push herself up on the pillows.

"Avery, what God lets happen doesn't change Who He is. He is always righteous—He always wants what is right. I'm the one who made the mistake, not God."

"Yeah, well, God could've stopped it!" Avery shot back.

"Dad says that because of this accident, I will think twice about how I drive in a heavy rainstorm. I should have been home before dark. I didn't see the other car coming, and I got hit because of my poor choices. Within a week, I'll be back on my feet again. However, I will never forget the lesson I've learned. No, Avery, God wanted the right thing, which was for me to be home before it was dark. I'm glad He is using my mistake to help me become wiser."

"I guess that makes sense, and I'm glad you're going to be okay," Avery said as she gently hugged her sister. "I'll leave you now, so you can get some more sleep."

For the LORD is righteous...

Psalm 11:7a

What About You?

Are there times when you question God's righteousness when it is really something you've done wrong?

Like...

- When you ride your bike with no shoes, and you get angry at God that you have scraped your toe?
- When you forget to study for a test, and you get angry at God that you failed the test?
- When you forget to clean up your bedroom, and you get angry at God that you get grounded?

Take Time to Pray!

Confess your bad habit of blaming God when it is really you who has made the mistake. Ask God to help you see His righteousness in all situations.

Day 85

MY GOD IS MY RULER

Read: I Timothy 6:15

"Ms. Bracken, you look good when you don't have a cigarette hanging out of your mouth," Aaron observed as he plopped himself down at the kitchen table.

Trevor's mom shut the fridge door and leaned against it with a smirk. "Aaron, you're the only kid I know who would be so bold as to make a statement like that."

"Really, Mom?" Trevor asked as he pulled their afternoon snack out of the microwave. "Aaron prayed about your smoking, so he is as much a part of this as you and me."

"I guess so," Ms. Bracken said with a shrug as she walked to the kitchen sink and began making the orange juice from a can. "The truth is that nicotine ruled me; I was under its complete control. It feels good to be free."

"Yeah, I can believe that!" Aaron said without stopping to think. "There should only be one Ruler in your life, and that's God."

"Okay, Mr. March," Ms. Bracken said as she set the empty juice can on the counter. "You got me to quit smoking; are you now working on getting me saved?"

Aaron smiled as he popped his snack into his mouth. "You can't blame a guy for trying. I mean, look how good you feel because you decided to quit smoking."

Trevor's mom laughed.

"There is no end to how bold you can be," she said as she poured both boys a glass of orange juice.

"Let's just say you and Trevor are on my prayer list," Aaron shared.

Trevor looked up in surprise.

"Me, too?"

Aaron and Ms. Bracken laughed at the look on Trevor's face. Nodding his head, Aaron thanked Ms. Bracken for the snack and then pulled Trevor from the kitchen.

> *God, the blessed and only Ruler,*
> *the King of kings and Lord of lords.*
> *I Timothy 6:15*

What About You?

Many things can rule our lives besides God.
Like . . .

- Anger when you respond to difficulties with angry thoughts or words.

- Peer pressure when your friends' opinions influence you to make decisions.

- Insecurities when you don't like who you are because of what others say about you.

Take Time to Pray!

Say sorry to God for anything you allow to rule your life besides God. Tell God you want Him to be the Ruler of your life.

Day 86

MY GOD IS MY SAVIOR

Read: Isaiah 45:21

"Death to geography!" Aaron declared as his textbook tumbled from his bed. Trevor slammed his book closed in support of his friend's decree. Aaron sat up on his bed and peered over at Trevor, who was sprawled across Aaron's bedroom floor.

"Let's take a study break and shoot some hoops," Aaron suggested.

"That's been your best thought all afternoon," Trevor agreed as he jumped up and grabbed Aaron's ball sitting beside his closet.

For the next fifteen minutes, the two boys forgot all about their studies as they worked up a sweat playing basketball in Aaron's driveway.

"Yay!" Trevor cheered as the ball swished through the hoop. "I'm the winner of the first game. Want to play one more game before we go back to your room to study?"

"I'll play one more game, but I want to ask you a question first," Aaron stated.

"Okay, but make it quick; I don't want my winning streak to run out," Trevor said as he dribbled the ball from side to side.

"Did you know that your acceptance of Jesus as your Savior is at the top of my prayer list?"

"What does that mean—the top of your prayer list?" Trevor wondered.

"It means I pray for you first thing every morning. Jesus died to save you from the penalty of your own sin, remember? He paid the price, so you don't have to. That's why He's your Savior. You just need to accept the gift of salvation."

Trevor, not sure what he thought of Aaron's prayers, shot the ball at the hoop and missed.

"Oh great, I'm losing my touch as we stand here and talk," Trevor moaned.

"Fine, let's play," Aaron agreed as he grabbed the rebound. "Just remember, God hears my prayers. Your mom quit smoking; it's just a matter of time before you say yes to God!"

> *There is no God apart from me,*
> *a righteous God and a Savior; there is none but me.*
>
> Isaiah 45:21

What About You?

Are you praying for someone who needs to know Jesus as his or her Savior?

Like...

- A friend?
- A family member?
- An enemy because they need Jesus as their Savior, too?

Take Time to Pray!

Jesus encourages us to pray for everyone in our life who needs to know Jesus as his or her Savior. Start a prayer list today and begin to pray every day for those people in your life who still don't know Jesus as their Savior.

Day 87

MY GOD IS MY SHEPHERD

Read: Psalm 23

Sarah was back at school; and once again, the McPherson household returned to its regular routine. Saturday morning, Avery was up early, dressed, and ready for some time with Rio. As their car rolled up the stone drive leading to the stables, Avery and her mom were greeted with a funny sight.

"Mom, look at that fat goat with a bucket over her head. What has James gone and done now?"

Avery and her mom laughed at the goat's antics as she tried to remove the wedged bucket.

"She was probably trying to steal some grain and didn't take into account the small size of the bucket," Mom observed.

In the goat's efforts to dislodge the bucket, she ran into the side of the barn. Avery jumped from the car and ran to help the confused goat. Just as she pulled the bucket off the goat's head, James rounded the corner.

"Are you changing from a horse trainer to a goat shepherd, James? Well, you have your hands full with this one!" Avery laughed as the goat grabbed a halter and took off.

"No, there's no change in my career plans," James said as he chased the goat and grabbed the halter. "I'm goat-sitting for a week. It has only been one day; and already, I'm worn out. Being a shepherd is serious babysitting. Apparently, whether it is goats or sheep, they need protection and guidance all the time; otherwise, they get themselves into trouble."

Just then, a ripping sound, followed by a gush of grain, came from inside the barn. James and Avery ran into the barn to find a section of a grain bag clamped in the goat's teeth and the grain spilling all over the barn floor.

With a laugh, Avery gave James a pat on the back. "It's going to be a long week!"

> *The LORD is my shepherd, I lack nothing.*
> *Psalm 23:1*

What About You?

Jesus willingly wants to be our Shepherd. He wants to protect and guide us while keeping us out of trouble. Can you think of ways He does this in your life?

Like . . .

- Sending friends who give you good advice?
- Giving you parents who care for you?
- Giving you the Bible where you can find direction and guidance?

Take Time to Pray!

Say sorry to God for the times you have been like the goat, making God's job difficult because of the trouble you have gotten yourself into. Thank Him for being the Good Shepherd.

Day 88
MY GOD IS MY SHIELD

Read: Psalm 28:7

A rumble in Kaylin's stomach sent her in search of something to eat. Bounding down the stairs and crossing the living room, she entered the kitchen and threw open the fridge. Thankfully, she found some milk, eggs, and cheese. A few minutes later, Kaylin slid her cheesy eggs onto her plate, removed the tea towel from her shoulder, and put the pan in the sink.

She was walking out of the kitchen when an odd smell caused her to look back at the stove. The smoking tea towel was lying over the stove's element that she had forgotten to turn off. The towel burst into flames as Kaylin grabbed some tongs and used them to fling the flaming towel into the sink; then she doused it with water. Shaking all over, Kaylin sank to the floor and began to cry.

"Dear Lord," she said through sobs, "I could have burned down the apartment. Thanks for letting me smell the smoke and helping me to act fast. Thanks for shielding me from the flames. Now, please shield me from my parents' anger."

Just as she finished her prayer, she heard the front door open; and her mom cried out in panic, "Fire!"

"Mom, it's okay. I put it out."

Her parents rushed around the corner to find Kaylin rising from the floor, her face streaked with tears. Her dad's face grew red as he stormed over to the sink. But before he could begin to yell, Kaylin's mom put out a hand to silence him.

Calmly, she asked, "Kaylin, are you okay?"

Shocked at the care in her mom's voice, she just nodded.

"Why don't you take your eggs upstairs, and I will clean up this mess?"

Stunned by the kindness, Kaylin grabbed the bowl and left the kitchen. On the way upstairs, she thanked God for being her Shield and Protector against her parent's anger and the flames.

> *The LORD is my strength and my shield...*
> *Psalm 28:7a*

What About You?

Are you quick to ask God to protect you, to shield you from something that might hurt you?

Like...

- When a bully at school keeps messing with you?

- When a neighbor keeps blaming you for something you didn't do?

- When a sister or brother is in the habit of calling you names?

Take Time to Pray!

Now is a good time to thank God for being your Shield. Ask Him to help you to notice when He protects you.

Day 89

MY GOD IS SOVEREIGN

Read: Revelation 6:10

The students at Glenwood School crowded into the auditorium for a general assembly. Before the guest speaker was called to the podium, Mr. Davis, their principal, had a few words to say.

"Students of Glenwood," Mr. Davis bellowed, "I, your fearless leader, rule this school with all the power that being a principal can give me."

Mr. Davis cleared his throat before he continued, giving Aaron a moment to make a crack in Trevor's ear. "Mr. Davis is turning red while trying to keep his voice booming. Who is he trying to impress?"

Trevor shrugged as Mr. Davis continued, "As sovereign of this great school, it is my duty to make sure you get a well-rounded education. Today, I've invited Ms. Mother Nature to speak to you about keeping our planet green."

On cue, a woman covered in leaves emerged from the side of the stage and wiggled her way to the podium amid laughter from the entire student body. Mother Nature's voice was the exact opposite of Mr. Davis' voice. She squeaked out her introduction, but most of the students missed it because there was so much laughter. "Green is good; that is my chant. Grow a tree, smell a flower, love the green grass that makes beautiful lawns . . . "

Kaylin was into recycling, but this woman was too much. Kaylin leaned over and whispered to Avery, "How long do you think it took her to glue those leaves in place?'

Avery responded between her giggles,
"I want to know what our sovereign leader was doing when he hired Ms. Mother Nature to speak to us. He is far from sovereign if he thinks she's going to motivate us to recycle."

Sovereign Lord, holy and true . . .
Revelation 6:10a

What About You?

Unlike Mr. Davis, God knows what is best for us; and He leads us to the best. That is why God is Sovereign above all others!
Like . . .

- When He leads you to read the Bible.

- When He motivates you to go to youth group or church.

- When He provides you with friends who will help you get to know God better.

Take Time to Pray!

Thank God for being a good Sovereign, Who is above all others!

Day 90
MY GOD IS MY STRENGTH

Read: Habakkuk 3:19

Mr. Davis, the students' so-called sovereign leader, finished his interruption over the intercom, leaving Ms. Phillips' math class nervously awaiting their final exam.

Ms. Phillips stood like a sergeant at the front of the class. "Okay, students, notebooks under your chairs. You should have two sharpened pencils on your desk and your hands in your lap. I will begin passing out the exam."

Trevor had his hands clasped together so tightly that his knuckles were turning white. He decided to use the minute he had while waiting to receive the exam to try something new.

God, Trevor began, *this is Trevor. I know I've never prayed like this before, but, boy, could I use some help. I've studied, but I stink at math. Oh, I guess You already know that. Well, give me the strength to get through this and to remember everything I studied, okay?*

Trevor was forced to finish his silent prayer as Ms. Phillips laid the exam on his desk. As he picked up his pencil, Trevor noticed that his hand was no longer shaking.

Hmmm, Trevor wondered to himself, *maybe this praying thing is something I should have tried sooner!*

The Sovereign LORD is my strength . . .

Habakkuk 3:19a

What About You?

God is so strong! Have you ever asked Him to share His strength with you?

Like...

- When you are trying to break a bad habit?
- When you know you need to tell the truth?
- When you need to finish a job that you find difficult?

Take Time to Pray!

Where do you need God's strength? Ask Him for that strength right now!

Day 91

MY GOD IS MY TEACHER

Read: Isaiah 48:17

The school bell rang, and the students of Glenwood erupted through the front doors cheering. The last day of school brought a smile to everybody's face. Backpacks were flying in the air; guys were calling to each other; and girls were hugging. Summertime had finally arrived.

The four friends emerged from school together.

Avery raised her voice above the noise. "My mom is picking me up, and she said she would give each of you a ride home."

"Great," said Aaron, "the sooner I start summer, the better."

Avery slid into the front seat as the other three filled the back seat.

"Glad school is over, kids?" Avery's mom asked with a smile as she pulled onto the road.

"Yeah," all four chimed in together.

"No more teachers, no more exams," Trevor sighed with relief. "Basketball, softball, soccer, and Mickey will be filling my summer!"

"Now, wait a minute," Kaylin stopped Trevor. "After all we've been through this school year, we all have to agree to keep one teacher in our lives this summer."

"Not Fussy Phillips!" Aaron declared.

Everybody laughed at the horror in Aaron's eyes.

"No, the one Teacher we need to keep in our lives is always kind, loving, patient, and gentle," Kaylin explained.

"And he teaches at Glenwood?" Trevor asked in confusion.

"Well," Kaylin thought for a moment, "He wants to teach there."

"Kaylin," Trevor snapped, "what are you talking about?"

Mrs. McPherson thought she better step in to support Kaylin. "I think she's talking about God. He is the greatest Teacher ever."

"Oh, that's a relief," Trevor said, dropping back against the car seat. "I thought you were hinting at summer school!"

> *I am the LORD your God, who teaches you what is best for you . . .*
> *Isaiah 48:17*

What About You?

What lesson is God trying to teach you, inside or outside of school? Like . . .

- Honesty is the best policy (Eph. 4:25)?

- "Do to others what you would have them do to you" (Matt. 7:12)?

- "Be quick to listen, slow to speak and slow to become angry" (James 1:19).

Take Time to Pray!

Choose one lesson you need to work on then ask God to help you to be quick to learn that lesson.

Day 92

MY GOD IS TRUSTWORTHY

Read: II Samuel 7:28

The phone buzzed early Saturday morning, waking Kaylin from a sound sleep.

"Hello?" Kaylin's groggy voice sounded into the phone.

"Kaylin, honey, it's me, Christi, from next door. I'm sorry if I woke you."

"It's okay, Christi; it's only Saturday and the first day of the summer holiday."

Christi laughed into the phone.

"I'm glad you haven't lost your sense of humor with such a rude awakening, but I'm calling so early because I need you to babysit all day. Late last night, my boss set an emergency meeting for today. McCall wants you to babysit, of course, and you're the one I trust the most to look after McCall while you have fun with her."

"Okay, when do you need me?" Kaylin asked as she sat up in bed to stretch.

"In ten minutes . . ."

"What?" Kaylin's eyes shot open as she jumped from her bed. "I have to hang up, and don't expect me to look great."

Kaylin clicked off the phone and ran into her bathroom. Twelve minutes later, Kaylin, with her shoes in one hand and her makeup case in the other, stood before McCall's door, waiting for it to open.

"Kaylin!" McCall threw herself into her babysitter's arms as Kaylin struggled to get inside the apartment.

"Thanks, Kaylin," Christi called from the landing that overlooked their living room.

A moment later, Christi came running down the steps, her arms loaded with books and folders. "Kaylin, I've left two hundred dollars on the kitchen table. Spend it all if you want to. McCall has many ideas to fill the day—take a taxi, go out to lunch, and enjoy your first day of summer."

As Christi ran down the hall toward the elevator, Kaylin called after her, "Two hundred dollars is a lot of money! Are you sure?"

As the elevator doors closed, Kaylin heard Christi calling, "I'm sure! I trust you!"

> *God! Your covenant is trustworthy . . .*
> *II Samuel 7:28*

What About You?

We know God is trustworthy all the time; but as you become more like Jesus, are you becoming more trustworthy?

Like . . .

- Making sure you do good work when you are finishing a task?
- Telling the truth, even in tough situations?
- Always being honest with money?

Take Time to Pray!

Confess the times when you have been less than trustworthy. Ask God to help you to become more like Jesus, Who is trustworthy, no matter what!

Day 93
MY GOD IS TRUTH

Read: Psalm 25:5

Aaron swung open Trevor's screen door, knowing Ms. Bracken was waitressing at the restaurant and Trevor was home alone.

"Trev," he called out, "I'm here early. Come on, let's go practice our passing before the other guys show up at the field for the soccer game."

Trevor came around the corner blowing his nose. "Sorry, Aaron, I'm sick; you'll have to go without me."

"Does this have anything to do with the last practice when you missed the ball and fell in front of all the guys?"

Trevor shook his head as he blew his nose again. "Nah, go on without me."

"Fine, hope you feel better," Aaron said with a sigh, letting the screen door slam behind him.

Trevor watched Aaron walk down his driveway; then he threw the tissue away and began to laugh.

"Come here, Mickey!" His dog jumped off the living room chair wagging his tail and ready to play. "Aaron fell for it. How gullible can a best friend be? Now I have all afternoon to teach you to fetch."

Trevor chuckled while rubbing Mickey's neck.

Aaron's voice startled Trevor. "I don't know how gullible most best friends are, but I trusted you to tell me the truth. I guess that was my mistake. By the way, I came back for the soccer ball."

Trevor dropped his head. "I'm sorry, Aaron. It was easier to lie than to tell you how embarrassed I was at the practice. I don't want to face the guys."

"Trev," Aaron said, stepping inside the house, "they've forgotten it. Besides, you make tons of great plays and only a few bad ones, but you always come out ahead. Truth is too important to sacrifice because you are embarrassed. God always gives us the truth, and He expects truth in return."

"Will you forgive me?" Trevor asked.

"Only if you get dressed and come play."

"Okay, Mickey, go lie down, boy. I've got a soccer game to go to."

Guide me in your truth and teach me, for you are God my Savior . . .
Psalm 25:5

What About You?

Every word from God's mouth is the truth. Can you say the same about the words that come out of your mouth?

Like . . .

- When you exaggerate?
- When you tell a little white lie?
- When you avoid sharing some information you know needs to be shared?

Take Time to Pray!

Telling the truth is always the best choice. Ask God to help you always tell the truth.

Day 94

MY GOD IS UNFAILING

Read: Psalm 36:7

Avery was sad that this Sunday would be the last small group story time she would teach for the season. Summertime church attendance was small enough that the children up to fifth grade all gathered as one big group, so Avery had the summer off.

Avery's thoughts were brought to a sudden halt as Billy raced around the corner and bumped into her.

"Eager to get to Kid's Community, Billy?" Avery giggled.

Billy's freckled face and toothless grin beamed up at Avery. "No, I'm running from a girl who is chasing me!"

Avery pretended to be horrified. "Well, we don't want any of that. Why don't you help me get ready for the class? You can be my assistant."

"Do assistants get paid?" Billy wondered as he picked up the scissors.

"No, not in money, but if you cut out these red circles, I'll give you an extra candy," Avery promised.

Billy nodded, ready to take his job seriously.

Avery thought she would try out part of her lesson on Billy right now; so as he finished his last circle, she cried out, "Great success, great success!"

"Teacher, they're just circles!" Billy looked confused.

"Do you know what success is, Billy?"

"No."

"It's doing what you had hoped to do."

"Oh."

"Do you know what failing is?"
"Yeah, it's when I get put in time-out!"
Avery laughed.
"Yeah, you've got the idea. Does God ever fail?"
"No, who would put God in time-out?" Billy wondered.
"Nobody would," Avery acknowledged. "He is God, and He is always a success. The Bible says God is unfailing. But I like the way you said it—God never needs a time-out."

Ruffling Billy's red hair, Avery handed him a candy for his great success in cutting circles.

> *How priceless is your unfailing love, O God ...*
> *Psalm 36:7*

What About You?

Are there times when you fail?
Like...

- When you take a test at school?

- When you don't control your tongue and end up saying something bad?

- When you are expected to do a job but don't end up doing it?

Take Time to Pray!

Thank God that He is unfailing in His love, patience, trust, care, compassion, and so much more.

Day 95

MY GOD IS UPRIGHT

Read: Psalm 92:15

The Bridge was crazy fun all night. Avery won the splash dunking contest, and Trevor ended up eating the most donuts in sixty seconds. At the end of the night, Steve settled the group down for one important announcement.

"Here's the deal," Steve began. "We leave for camp next Saturday. The available spots have been full for a while, but one spot has opened. If someone here would still like to go, you need to let me know and get the money to me as soon as possible." Steve closed in prayer, and then everybody started to talk.

Aaron tugged on Trevor's sleeve.

"Hey, this is your opportunity. Grab the application and start begging your mom for some money."

Kaylin and Avery walked toward the two guys, and Kaylin dangled a piece of paper in Trevor's face.

"For you. I got you the camp form, so now you have no excuses."

Trevor screwed up his face as he shook his head. "I know; I know. I'll bring it home, but it will take a miracle for my mom to say yes and give me the money needed to go to camp."

"Try that praying thing again, Trev!" Aaron suggested.

Trevor grabbed the sheet from Kaylin's hand.

"Can't hurt to pray. Can't hurt to ask. But it could all be God's joke on me."

"What?" all three asked at once.

"Yeah, to mess with me, you know—a spot opens up; my mom says yes; but the spot is filled before I get the money in to Steve."

"Hey," Avery said, "my God isn't mean like that. He's upright in all He does. If it is God's plan for you to go to camp, everything will work out. Now, go ask your mom and trust God to do what is best for you."

The LORD is upright . . .

Psalm 92:15

What About You?

God is upright in all He does, but there might be times when you feel He might be playing some kind of joke on you.

Like . . .

- When you pray for a spot on the team but don't make the team?
- When you pray for someone to get better but they get worse?
- When you pray for a new friend but still feel all alone?

Take Time to Pray!

God's plans are upright—good and trustworthy. But sometimes, we don't understand them. As you pray, ask God to help you to be patient as you wait to see what His best is for your life. Maybe being on the team might distract you from your schoolwork. Maybe someone's sickness will give them an opportunity to tell others about God's love. Maybe God wants you alone for a while so that you decide to make Him your Best Friend. Ask God to help you to trust that all His ways are upright, and then ask God to help you make wise choices as His upright plan unfolds for you.

Day 96

MY GOD IS VICTORIOUS

Read: I Corinthians 15:57

Trevor walked through his front door, letting the screen door slam behind him. His mother looked up from the TV and smiled at her son.

"Have fun at The Bridge?" she asked as she clicked off the TV.

"I ate the most donuts in sixty seconds," Trevor bragged as he dropped the folded sheet on the coffee table.

"What's this?" his mom asked as she opened the piece of paper in front of her.

"I have the chance to go to camp for a week. I want to go, but it will cost $120. I have forty dollars in my top drawer. I could put it toward the cost, but that still means you'll have to pay eighty dollars."

Trevor dropped onto the living room chair across from his mom. His mom reached into the pocket of her waitressing uniform and pulled out a wad of cash.

"Well, I had an unusually good night tonight with my tips. One man gave me a very large tip and said, 'Do a good deed with that money.' Guess how much my tips totaled tonight?"

"I don't know—twenty dollars?"

"Trevor, the tips totaled exactly eighty dollars!"

Trevor looked stunned as he stared back at his mother.

"Trev, I'm beginning to think that Aaron's God is really interested in our lives. I know I have been fighting against Him, but who knows? He might just win."

"Yes!" Trevor cheered as he jumped from the living room chair and gave his mom a big hug. "This is tons better than winning the donut-eating contest. Wait 'til I tell Aaron that God is winning you over to His side." Trevor turned to head for his room when he had another thought. "Mom, can we take the money to Steve first thing tomorrow? I want to make sure I get that last spot."

"You bet!" she said with a smile.

> *But thanks be to God! He gives us the victory through our Lord Jesus Christ.*
>
> I Corinthians 15:57

What About You?

In the end, God wins. He is always victorious; but sometimes, we have trouble seeing God's victories.

Like . . .

- When our view on winning looks different from God's view of winning.
- When we want our own way, not God's way.
- When we don't wait long enough to see the victory.

Take Time to Pray!

Do you have a prayer request that you are asking God where you want Him to win, to get His way? Ask God to help you to have His view of victory. Ask God to help you to be patient for the victory God will eventually bring.

Day 97
MY GOD IS WISE

Read: Romans 16:27

The front door of Kaylin's condo closed behind her parents, leaving her standing alone in the middle of the living room. "Great, I guess I'm packing for camp on my own."

Kaylin's words hung unanswered in the empty apartment. With a shrug, she clomped up the stairs to begin sorting through her clothes for camp. *What should I pack*, wondered Kaylin.

Just then, her phone buzzed.

Aaron was on the other end of the phone when Kaylin answered. "Hey, this is a surprise," Kaylin remarked. "Is everything okay?"

"Yeah, I wanted to call you, Trevor, and Avery to remind you guys to pack a jacket 'cause the nights are cool and to make sure you have your toothbrush and, well, your bathing suit and stuff."

Kaylin began to laugh. "Well, aren't you the wise father checking up on his kids."

"Nah, it's nothing like that. I'm just so excited about camp, and I want everyone to have a good time."

"No need to worry, *Dad*—I have it all packed!" Kaylin hung up with another chuckle as she rushed downstairs to grab her jacket from the front hall closet. Maybe it was a good thing Aaron had called. Shutting the closet door, Kaylin noticed her sunglasses on the coffee table and decided it would be wise to take them, too. With a dive-and-roll, she launched over the back of the couch, rolled over the seat, and landed beside the table with a thud. With the momentum, Kaylin knocked the table, and the ugly statue of the goddess toppled to the floor. Kaylin picked up the statue, only to find three of the arms had broken off.

"Ugh, that wasn't too wise of me. I don't mind that this useless goddess is broken, but my mom is going to freak out!" With a roll of her eyes, Kaylin put the goddess and her missing arms back on the table. "Well, maybe this foolish thing will be gone when I get home from camp."

To the only wise God be glory forever through Jesus Christ! Amen.
Romans 16:27

What About You?

Our wise God always knows what you need and what is best for you to do. Do you remember to ask God for His wisdom?
Like...

- When you are about to make a decision?
- When you have to make a choice?
- When you are unsure about what you need to do next?

Take Time to Pray!

Thank God for being a wise God. Then ask Him to help you to make wise decisions.

Day 98

MY GOD IS WONDERFUL

Read: Isaiah 9:6

The four friends tumbled out of Mrs. McPherson's car and retrieved their sleeping bags and suitcases. Avery grabbed her pink pillow from the back seat; and Trevor tugged on his ball cap, making sure it was firmly in place. They were ready to find their cabins and settle in for a wonderful week at camp.

Trevor and Aaron were in the last of the boys' cabins called Mighty Warriors. On the other side of the grove of trees was a collection of girls' cabins. Avery and Kaylin quickly discovered they were in the Prince of Peace cabin. After meeting their cabin leader and a few of their cabin mates, they heard a whistling sound, followed by an announcement that they were to head to the playing field.

"Hey," said Aaron, "there are the girls. Let's see if they found their cabin."

Kaylin waved to the guys, then gave a thumbs-up, indicating that all was good. However, they didn't have time to talk because the camp leader was introducing himself.

"Welcome to camp. You are in for a great week. I will be on the grounds if you need anything, but my assistant for this week will be leading the fun. Let me introduce you to Steve."

A cheer went up from the four friends when they realized their own youth leader was going to be leading all the fun for the week.

"Are you all ready for a wonderful week?" Steve called to the crowd of campers.

A cheer erupted from the campers.

"Well, let's get started on our first activity. Pair up and get ready to go on a scavenger hunt. When I blow the whistle, come up and grab the list and your collection bag. You have fifteen minutes to find as many things on the list as you can. When the whistle blows again, get back here with what you have found."

The whistle sounded; sheets and bags were grabbed; pairs went running; and laughter and cheers sounded from the edges of the playing field. Hidden in the grass were all sorts of wrapped candies. The campers found two of each scattered here and there; and fifteen minutes later, everyone had a bag full of treats.

Avery peered into her bag of treats and whispered to Kaylin, "What a wonder-licious way to start a week of camp!"

> *And he will be called Wonderful Counselor...*
> *Isaiah 9:6*

What About You?

We often use the word wonderful for things that make us happy and are good. In the Bible, we see that God's "plan is wonderful" (Isa. 28:29), that He has "done wonderful things" (Isa. 25:1), and that He is a "Wonderful Counselor" (Isa. 9:6). How is He a wonderful God to you?

Like...

- When you see your plans becoming a reality?
- When you hear kind and encouraging words that make you smile?
- When your parents give you advice that you know is good.

Take Time to Pray!

Tell God how wonderful He is! Be specific!

Day 99
MY GOD IS WORTHY

Read: I Chronicles 16:25-27

Camp was turning out to be the best week of Trevor's life. He and Aaron saw Kaylin and Avery at the paddleboard competition and the joint barbecue; but the last night, the boys were on their own. They gathered at Campfire Point for the last service. Trevor felt a warmth inside as the worship band led the songs from the front. Trevor especially loved the song, "Worthy of It All."

When the boys all sat down, the camp director stood in front of the bonfire and began his talk. "All right, guys, tell me all the things for which God is worthy."

From all over, the campers called out their answers: "Praise, honor, love, devotion, worship, trust . . . "

Trevor sat back and thought about all God had done for him this past year. God had helped him and his mom, and things were so much better. Trevor's attention was drawn back to the front as the camp director continued to speak.

"Our God is a zealous God Who is worthy of all you have to offer Him," the camp director explained. "God is devoted to a purpose, and His purpose is to save you. God won't give up until you say yes to Him!"

Suddenly, Trevor needed to be alone. He slid from beside Aaron and walked to the back of the group. Pulling Steve aside, Trevor explained that he wanted to talk alone with God for a few minutes.

Steve pointed down the dirt path leading through the trees to the beach area.

"Tell you what," Steve said, "if you settle yourself on the dock, you can have some alone time with God. I will still be able to see you while I am here with the group."

"Thanks," Trevor said as he turned and made his way to the dock. Just before he settled in for his talk with God, Trevor looked back to see Steve waving at him from the other end of the path.

For great is the Lord and most worthy of praise . . .
I Chronicles 16:25

What About You?

When you get alone with God, do you ever stop to think about all the ways God is worthy?

Like . . .

- Being worthy of your worship?
- Being worthy of your trust?
- Being worthy of your love?

Take Time to Pray!

Worship God right now by telling Him all the ways He is special.

Day 100
MY GOD IS ZEALOUS

Read: Ezekiel 39:25

Trevor laid on the dock staring up at the star-speckled sky. The words of the camp director were echoing in his head. *"Our God is a zealous God, Who is worthy of all you have to offer Him. God is devoted to a purpose, and His purpose is to save you. God won't give up until you say yes to Him!"*

All year long, Aaron had been bugging him to say yes to God, and Trevor knew it was time to do something about it. As Trevor sat up on the dock, he heard the boys singing the final song before going to the snack shack. He was glad Steve had let him have these few minutes alone to talk with God. Running his fingers through his hair, Trevor straightened his shoulders, ready to pray the most important prayer of his life.

"God, You don't give up. The fact that You are devoted to me when my own dad isn't devoted to me seems weird, but I want to thank You for Your devotion. You have given me the best gift ever—life through Jesus Christ. Thanks for letting Jesus die for my sins. I'm sorry You had to do that—I'm sorry I have sinned—I want Your forgiveness and salvation." Trevor finished his prayer with a big smile on his face. "Boy, do I feel better. I'll have to try this praying thing more often!"

Suddenly, Trevor realized the singing had stopped, and he knew he needed to get moving if he wanted to visit the snack shack. As he jumped off the dock onto dry sand, Trevor noticed a group of guys coming down the path. Aaron was in the lead.

"Hey, Aaron!" Trevor called.

Aaron nodded at Trevor and then told the other guys they would catch up to them at the shack.

"What happened? Is somethin' wrong?" Aaron wondered.

"No, I've never been happier!"

"Why? What happened?" Aaron asked, looking sideways at his smiling friend.

"Come on," said Trevor, "I'll tell you all about it on the way to the shack; I'm going to celebrate with a strawberry milkshake!"

> *Therefore, this is what the Sovereign LORD says...*
> *I will be zealous for my holy name.*
> Ezekiel 39:25

What About You?

To be zealous means to never give up. God is zealous for, passionate about, and committed to you. As you end these devotionals, what one thing is God still trying to teach you that He will continue to try to teach you until you learn it?

Like...

- Saying yes to God the way Trevor did?
- Learning to pray when things go wrong?
- Knowing God has a character quality that meets every one of your needs?

Take Time to Pray!

Ask God to continue to remind you of your need to learn what He wants you to learn. Thank Him for being zealous for you.

About the Author

As a devout follower of Christ, Mary-Lynn Chambers has always been passionate about teaching the Scriptures to others. During her years of full-time ministry in the church alongside her husband, Mary-Lynn published her first children's devotional, *A Time for Training Wheels* (available on Bible.org). Dr. Chambers' passion to write was enhanced further when she pursued her doctoral studies in English. She presently teaches English at a university, where her faith helps to inspire her students' love of literature. Her grandchildren have grown up listening to Mary-Lynn's stories. Now that some are in their preteen years, Mary-Lynn has designed a devotional that will engage preteen readers while inspiring a deeper understand of our great God.

Ambassador International's mission is to magnify the Lord Jesus Christ and promote His Gospel through the written word.

We believe through the publication of Christian literature, Jesus Christ and His Word will be exalted, believers will be strengthened in their walk with Him, and the lost will be directed to Jesus Christ as the only way of salvation.

For more information about
AMBASSADOR INTERNATIONAL
please visit:

www.ambassador-international.com
@AmbassadorIntl
www.facebook.com/AmbassadorIntl

Thank you for reading this book.

*Please consider leaving us a
review on your social media, favorite retailer's website,
Goodreads or Bookbub, or our website,
and check out the books on the following page.*

Also Available from Ambassador International

When King Solon banishes his once-faithful servant, Raphical, from his kingdom forever, Raphical sets out to destroy the mighty king and take down everyone who follows him, including Solon's son, Zarias.

In the peaceful kingdom of Ryecliff, the people live in harmony under the rule of the kind King William I and Queen Leandra. But when darkness threatens to take down the city, each person will have to choose for themselves in whose kingdom they wish to reside—Solon's or Raphical's.

Everyone will soon find their faith shaken, their wills tested, and their true characters revealed. In the end, the question will be who is left standing and who is the one true ruler of them all?

All Zeke wants to do is make it through school without attracting too much notice; after all, it isn't the teachers but a gang of bullies who run the school. He is one of the smartest kids in middle school and on the shorter side of average height. This, added to the fact that he has no friends since he moved, makes Zeke stand out as an easy target to the gang's unwelcome attention. One afternoon, as he walks home, he discovers an old box blending in with a pile of trash. Curiosity gets the better of Zeke, and he takes the box home. Little does he know that it holds the key to life-changing truths.

www.ingramcontent.com/pod-product-compliance
Lightning Source LLC
Chambersburg PA
CBHW062157080426
42734CB00010B/1727